PANEL CRAFT

by

Tommy Sandham

First Published in September, 1987 by **WILLOW PUBLISHING (MAGOR)**, Barecroft Common, Magor, Newport, Gwent, NP6 3EB

British Library Cataloguing in Publication Data

Sandham, Tommy
    Panel Craft: Featuring Ford Cortina
    MK.1 bodyshell restoration.
    1. Automobiles — Conservation and
    restoration — Amateur's manuals
    I. Title
    629.28'722   TL152.2
ISBN 0 − 9512523 − 0 − 5

Design, layout, text and most photography by the author.

Additional photographs by Susan Sandham, Roger Raisey, Roger Turner, Mark and Terry Hill, A.G. Coates.

Photographic services by Morris Ffitchett.

Production by Mopok Graphics, 128 Pikes Lane, Glossop, Derbyshire, SK13 8EH

Printed in England.

CONTENTS

INTRODUCTION

April, 1960 and Thomas Sandham senior stands beside his new Ford Anglia 105E, won in the Kelvin Hall, Glasgow. The author is behind the wheel, while his younger brother Peter fills the passenger seat. The arrival of this car sparked off the author's interest in Fords.

I've always been interested in things mechanical, as far back as I can remember, but I can date my special interest in Fords almost to the hour. On 30th April, 1960 my father won a brand new, shiny Ford Anglia 105E in a competition at the Kelvin Hall, Glasgow. From then on, I was hooked. (The number of the Anglia was 420 AGD, but I don't think it survived).

Later, in September 1962 he traded the Anglia for the latest Ford, and took delivery of one of the very first MKI Cortinas (14 GGE). I bought this car from my father a few years later and began to learn welding and metalwork. This interest has continued to date.

Early results were not very encouraging, but over the years I improved. Each time I bought a car, I tried different and more advanced things, such as building a Volvo pick-up from a crashed saloon, until now I can tackle almost any body job with reasonable confidence.

Over the years I kept looking for books that would tell me what I wanted to know, but they either described expensive, professional jigs for straightening wrecked cars, or they went to the other extreme and showed you how to repair everything by applying great lumps of plastic filler.

This book is different. I've tried to write what a newcomer to body repairs and restoration will want to know, and I've tried to write in a friendly style, much as I would say it, as if I was actually showing you what to do in my garage. To illustrate all the techniques described in the book, I've featured a photo-spread of a Ford Cortina MKI bodyshell undergoing a do-it-yourself restoration to become a useful drive to work car.

I have tried to remember the things I got stuck on — the things that caused me frustration because I knew they could be done, but I did not know how to do them.

In these pages I'll guide you through all

the common welding jobs including repair and replacement of: sills, floors, chassis/ frame legs, chassis/frame outriggers and much, much more. There is advice too on patching everything from wings to main frames and chassis. And by patching I mean a plate which will look smart and tidy and one you won't notice after a paint job.

I've had to assume that you cannot weld. I recommend the oxy-acetylene torch as the best all-round tool. There are many other devices on the market now, but the good old traditional torch is still the most versatile. If you can master the oxy-acetylene torch, you have learned a useful skill for life.

Just think! If you could weld and do body repairs it would open up a whole new group of restorable cars to you. You may only want to learn welding and bodywork techniques to restore one car, or you might be more ambitious and have ideas of starting a small business. Either way, Panel Craft can help you.

Most of what is described in Panel Craft is applicable to any car up to about 1970. After that time a new type of steel was used for bodywork. Called 'High Strength Steel' it requires a special welding technique not covered in this book. So, Panel Craft applies to cars and light commercials up to 1970. (There are a lot of people who would argue that after 1970 there is nothing worth restoring anyway!)

Don't let all this talk of Ford Cortinas put you off. Even if you are not a Ford fan, the information in this book can be applied to any steel-bodied car. There is currently a lot of interest in Britain centred on the Morris Minor as a 'durable' car which can

be rebuilt in a controlled way over a number of years. If this is the sort of thing you have in mind, then Panel Craft will help you to apply a similar formula to almost any other old car, regardless of year, make or model.

At the end of the book I invite you to have a browse through my bookshelves in the Bibliography section. I have a collection of metalwork, bodywork, panel beating, and car restoring books, some of which you may find useful.

As I write this introduction I am aware that by a curious coincidence the publication date of this book will mark the 25th

anniversary of the Cortina, born September 1962. In some small way I hope I have marked a motoring milestone, and at the same time helped other enthusiasts to save some cars from the scrap heap. There are still plenty of MKI Cortinas around waiting to be restored, but in a few years the non-restored ones will be gone for ever.

So, without any more introduction, let me say how much I have enjoyed researching and writing this book. I am still learning Panel Craft, although I have been practising since the early 1960s. I hope you find it interesting.

Good luck, and happy restoring!

TOMMY SANDHAM

MAGOR, SOUTH WALES
JULY, 1987.

This ex-Roger Clark rally Cortina created a lot of interest when it was displayed at Hagley Hall in 1986. I can hardly believe that 25 years have passed since the first Cortina was built. Must be getting old!

Basic Metal Shaping

The sleek lines of this Citroen show what shapes can be made out of sheet metal. Look closely at the curves and bends, and you will start to appreciate 'shape' in body panels.

Before we launch straight into metal bending and making your own repair panels, it is as well to set the scene which currently exists in the 'old car' movement. If you have intentions of restoring an old car, you may find it useful to know.

There are various one-make clubs which have been established for a number of years. They collect spare parts for their particular cars, as and when they become available. When supplies of certain items start to dry up, the clubs have to decide whether to re-manufacture them. This can be spectacularly expensive.

Items that could be bought for a few pounds when the car was new, can now cost over £100. For example, front wings used to be available in the 1960s for about £15. Over the years the demand dropped and the manufacturer decides at a certain point to make one last batch for all time. After that – no more!

These parts are then available for a number of years, with some far-sighted enthusiasts salting them away for the fu-ture. However, to do this on any large scale is not worth the investment. To tie up thousands of pounds in old body panels would not be looked on too favourably by the Financial Institutions. Panels take up a lot of storage space, and there is no guaran-tee that in ten or twenty years time you will be able to sell them. This is why main dealers clear out their stockrooms every so often. A part not selling is space wasted and dead money.

So, to return to the one-make clubs. They decide that their members need to have front wings. They contact the manufac-turer and find that the tool to make the wings went to the scrapyard/ crusher years ago. A tool can be made again, using a wing as a pattern, but it will cost thou-sands of pounds. The club has to make a decision: invest its spares fund in the front wings and hope that clubmembers will support it, or say, 'What the heck, when they're gone – they're gone!'

If the club decides to re-manufacture the item it has to try to sell some BEFORE they are made, to ease the cashflow. This means that the club members are being asked to fork out, say, £100 for an item that they might not need at that time. They are being asked for a financial com-mitment to the club. Many are unable to give it – for whatever reason. However, the club goes ahead and orders X – num-ber of items, knowing that it can only sell Y -number at the moment. The rest are put into store.

A similar situation exists with the small specialist dealer. He recognises a need for an item, costs it out, finds that he can just afford to have it re-manufactured and orders some.

For club and dealer, the next bit is the same, and equally unhappy for both. The car-owning public are entitled to shop around for the best buy. That is a basic right. However, if you want a new wing for your car and you know that the club/ dealer has them for £100, and you find one in an autojumble or Motor Factors shop for £20 – what do you do? It would be foolish to pay £100 if you can get it for £20. Both club and dealer lose.

Both club and dealer can win, if they find that the item will fit some other car as well as the one they made it for. The more potential customers, the better the chances of financial success. Without a profit to put back into the club or business, there will be no more parts made. In the case of front wings, they will only fit one particular model. Other items can fit several cars. For example some chassis parts with jacking points could be made so that they will fit several models. Similarly, door sealing rubbers might fit several widely-different cars. These avenues MUST be explored by the clubs and dealers. They must not be too disappointed if people don't support them.

The problem will be resolved in ten or twenty years time, when you next need the item. It will ONLY be available from the club/ dealer who made the investment NOW.

There are also some dealers around who are out to rip you off with shoddy goods which don't really fit. Beware.

What I am trying to emphasise is that today we have a choice, tomorrow there will be no choice. Without giving up your right to a bargain, support your club or dealer whenever possible.

So, there are still plenty of parts available but if you can't find what you need and can't adapt something from another car, you can probably make it yourself, or pay for someone to make it.

Having set the scene for you, lets get on with some metalwork.

Learning

As I mentioned in the introduction, I have been learning Panel Craft for over 20 years, and much of what I learned has been

Bits and pieces for old Fords assembled at Hagley Hall in 1986. There are sills for MKI and MK2 Cortinas and in the foreground a lower front panel for the MKI.

the hard way. Numerous disappointments helped me to find the best way for an amateur to tackle a particular job. Unfortunately, I did not do any metalwork at school and it was much later that I started

A bit rough round the edges perhaps, but a solid, reliable car. The author's two-door MKI awaiting further restoration work.

to learn.

A night-school gas-welding course really helped a lot, but the teacher did not know much about chassis welding so I had to find out myself, by trial and error. Luckily, you have this book to guide you through all the tricky bits which no-one else remembers to write down.

Without doubt the most useful thing I did was learn to weld. This allowed me to purchase some really cheap cars and repair them. Each one I worked on turned out better than the one before. Let me give you an example.

The best car I ever bought is my 1964 British Ford Cortina MK1. In the four years since I bought it, I have travelled over 40,000 miles and rebuilt most of the chassis. I admit it still looks a mess, because I haven't got round to fixing the wings and doors (my excuse is I have to take time out to write books!), but it is like new underneath, reliable, starts first time and is strong and durable.

My Cortina will feature a lot in the pho-

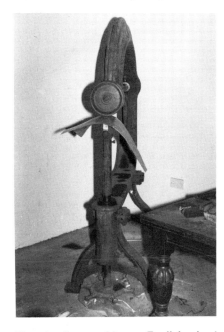

The wheeling machine or English wheel is the traditional tool for crafting body panels from sheet metal.

Can you rebuild this truck body? Compare this photo of the truck with the one on the next page.

tographs -- in fact you will see three of my Fords in the photographs. They are the 1964 Cortina mentioned already, which I bought in Blackpool for £60, plus a 1966 MK1 and a 1963 Ford Capri. The 1966 MKI cost me £30 and the Capri £25. Incidentally, I had to pay another £10 to get the MKI towed out of the field where it had been lying for six months!

At those sort of prices, you have to be prepared to work hard. But when you shut off the welding torch for the last time and start to apply paint, the car comes alive again and you know that it is all because of your efforts.

If I were to sum up Panel Craft, it would

This 1973 Chevrolet pick-up has rust damage on bumper and hood. Can you see how to repair the rust above the headlamp? Weld in a new piece. (Photo, Mark Hill).

be like this; 'You can patch, repair or replace, but the neater the job, the greater the satisfaction.'

Shape

Right from the start I want to get you thinking about 'shape' in metal. That is, the various curves and bends which you will find on any body panel. To illustrate this point, take a look at the photo of the truck on this page. I'm not sure what it is, but if I asked you to build a new body for this truck you probably wouldn't know where to begin. However, if you turn the page you will see the same photograph, but this time I've marked some lines on it. The lines indicate the changes in direction on

the various panels. Looks a whole different job now, doesn't it?

From now on, every time you look at any body panel, I want you to look at the shape. If you have to, mentally break it down into two, three or more shapes, until you arrive at the point where you say, 'I can make that'.

Every panel has some shape. If it did not have shape, it would be a flat piece of steel which would sag in the middle. Shape gives a panel strength and style. If rust takes the strength out of a panel, you still have the shape or style to show you how to repair it. All the way through this book I am going to remind you about shape. Its your number one guide in Panel Craft.

In later Chapters I'll show you how to tackle all the replacement and patching jobs you will ever need to do. Some you might find are too ambitious for you, others you can tackle easily. If you can run a decent weld, you can repair anything. Once you have done your first body job and discovered the pleasure it gives, you'll want to try more and more. Panel Craft can become addictive, so much so that I now find it more interesting than almost any mechanical work.

Keep thinking about 'shape' and each time you look at a car (like the one in front of you in the car park), compare its shape and style. More importantly, draw your own mental straight lines to split up the body panels into easily managed sections.

Now, I want to extend the idea of shape a bit further and show you how to create some of the basic shapes you will need during a restoration from a flat piece of steel. Just before we move into the garage and get our hands dirty, try this simple experiment.

First I want you to get a sheet of card, any sheet will do. Hold both ends of the sheet, one end in each hand. Now get someone to put a coin in the middle. Unless you have chosen very stiff card for the experiment, you should see the sheet of card sag in the middle. Experiment ends.

Now take the same sheet of card and lay it flat on a table. Push both ends of the card towards the middle, until it rises slightly. Now put the same coin on top of the raised area. You should see very little change in the shape of the card. It will probably take a few more coins before it will buckle under the weight.

What you have done in the second experiment is to give the sheet of card some shape. In doing this you have given it strength. You can see this simple principle used in packaging, where corrugated paper is used to pack objects and prevent them being damaged. Corrugated paper has shape, and is therefore stronger than a flat sheet of card. You can also see the principle applied to bridges, where a simple arch spans a river. The arch provides strength.

In the second experiment, the shape you created is known as a 'crown' and is widely used in body panels. If you make a more complex shape, you will add more

These lines indicate the major changes in shape. Although most of the panels are almost flat, the same principals apply to curved surfaces.

strength. However, the more complicated the shape, the harder it is for the power presses in the car factory to build the body. Strength can be created by simply putting a bend in the edge of a piece of steel.

Choice of Material

Having established that shape gives a panel strength, let's look at what to make the panel from. This book is about steel body panels. Some cars have aluminium bodies but they are usually expensive and require a lot of skill in restoring them. I have never had a car with aluminium body panels, although some of the early Lotus Cortinas had alloy boots, bonnets and door panels to reduce weight.

If you have severe accident damage like this — forget it. This book is not for you. That expensive jig and a lot of professional know-how are needed to straighten this 'totalled' car.

Sheet metal can be worked with a few basic tools, such as tin snips, hammer and dolly.

Aluminium is much easier to work than steel, as it is a softer material. It will bend more easily and can be shaped more easily. However, it is difficult to weld, especially for an amateur and will dent easily. It is also more expensive, and can scratch easily.

Steel is more difficult to shape, but is fairly easy to weld and can be bumped back into shape with simple tools and equipment. It is also a suitable material for use in heavy power presses, so manufacturers chose steel for their bodies.

If you are new to bodywork and are looking for a car to restore, don't make things difficult for yourself. Get yourself a tradition steel-bodied car — at least to start off with. Later, as your skills develop you can look towards something more exotic. Let's have a look at sheet steel in a little more detail.

Steel Thickness

Sheets of steel are available in different thicknesses for different jobs. Wait a minute, where do you buy this steel? First, ask at your local Motor Factor or the dealer who sells repair panels. He should have

Basic repair sections — flat pieces of steel with a right angled flange or lip.

Photo boards are common at car shows. They illustrate how the restoration was done and always attract a lot of attention. It pays to take photos as you do your restoration, even if you don't intend to exhibit the car.

stocks of sheet-metal in various sizes, and several gauges such as 18 and 20 gauge. If you don't have any success, try looking in the 'Yellow Pages' for 'Steel Stockholders' or 'Sheet Metal Workers'. These people often use large amounts of sheet steel, so it is well worth a visit to one of them and ask to see his scrap bin! I have often got some decent sized bits of scrap steel which are ideal for making repair panels. They don't charge you much for what they think is scrap!

For reference, the various gauges or thicknesses which you might need to use during metalworking are given below. Later in the book the various thicknesses will be discussed as they occur.

I suggest you take some time to discover sheet steel. What I mean is, I think you should handle pieces of it, weigh them in

Steel Thicknesses		
GAUGE NUMBER	SWG MMs	SWG INCHES
14	2.032	0.080
15	1.828	0.072
16	1.625	0.064
17	1.422	0.056
18	1.219	0.048
19	1.016	0.040
20	0.914	0.036
21	0.812	0.032
22	0.711	0.028

your hand, compare the weight of two similar sized pieces of steel of different thicknesses. Try bending a bit in your

The way to make those basic bends. This shows the use of an edge setter. The steel could also be held in a vice, or pliers. Getting a nice tidy bend is important for accurate results.

hand. Now try it with a thinner bit, then a thicker bit. After a little while you will start to notice the differences in weight and thickness. I'm not suggesting you need to be an expert, who can pick up a bit of scrap and tell me its thickness, chemical composition and country of origin. All I want is that you should be aware of differences in weight and thickness.

If you can get some pieces of scrap, ask the supplier to tell you what gauge it is. Then when you take it home to practice on, you will have a better idea of what you will be able to do with metalworking tools.

You can learn a lot of valuable lessons just by making some dents in a bit of scrap, then trying to tap them out again with a hammer and dolly. Similarly, try welding a few bits of scrap together, just to get the feel of the welding equipment. All the way through this book I will keep on suggesting you practice on some scrap first. That way you won't create a problem on your restoration project and become down-hearted. Even now, I sometimes try a shape out on a bit of scrap, knowing that it will be thrown away. The second attempt is ALWAYS 100% better. The best craftsman in the world had to start sometime.

Shaping

There are many ways to shape panel steel, including hammer and dolly, heat and hammer, wheeling machines, bending machines and so on. All these tools are described in the next Chapter, so don't

The lip is bent over a bit at a time until the right angle is formed. After you have done your best with the edge setter try....

worry if you are not too familiar with them. You will not be able to get your hands on all of these tools, but in the home workshop it is possible to make quite involved shapes if you are prepared to make them in separate parts. Remember where we mentally split a body panel into several parts? That was the theory, now for some practical work!

Lets start with a simple example. I say simple, because it looks simple to me now, but the first time I tried it, it seemed like a miracle.

Take a piece of sheet metal about six inches long, and perhaps about six or eight inches wide. I want you to make a 90 degree bend, (or lip) of about one half inch wide, along one edge of the piece of steel. Why? Because many frame or chassis parts have 90 degree lips so that they can be welded to floor sections. If you are going to restore chassis parts, you need to be able to make a 90 degree bend.

How do you do it? I'll tell you three ways – you can probably find some more for yourself.

Method 1:

Use a tool called an 'Edge Setter' which is described fully in the next Chapter. You can make a nice, neat, controlled bend using this simple little tool which you can

....the hammer and dolly. Here the edge is being 'dressed' against a dolly with a flat, straight edge.

make in about 5 minutes. You might find you have to hold the steel in a vice, or a pair of pliers, but often you can hold the steel in one hand and use the tool with the other. This is shown in the photograph.

Another way to bend steel. Put the steel in a vice, against a straight edge, and hammer the edge over. The tyre lever helps to spread the hammer blows.

Method 2:

Take a pair of pliers and fit the jaws over the edge of the panel steel. Grip the steel and rotate the pliers to make a bend. Move the pliers along an inch and make another bend. Continue to move the pliers and make bends. When you reach the end, you can often go over the bend again and get it over further. When you have got it over as far as you can with the pliers, get a hammer and dolly or similar straight edge and gently hammer the bend right over until it makes 90 degrees.

Method 3:

Lay the piece of steel against a flat piece of wood, so that the metal to be bent is overhanging the piece of wood. Now fit both the steel and piece of wood into a vice and do it up tight. Check that the steel is still in place and that the bend line is straight. Now, using a small hammer tap the overhanging piece of steel so that it starts to bend over towards the edge of the wood. Continue bending and tapping until the steel is bent at 90 degrees. Don't hit too hard otherwise something else will start to happen, which I will tell you about a little later on.

You have now bent your first piece of steel! No big deal you might think, but stick with me and I'll guide you through the more interesting bits. (By the way, in the above examples I did not tell you to mark a bend line on the steel. That was because it was just an exercise, and I wanted you to concentrate on the bending.

Later on, I'll show you how to mark out the shape you want).

Suppose you want to make another repair patch from a piece of steel, bent as above so that there are two sides of about one inch. It needs to be about six to eight inches long, the sort of shape you need to join two other pieces of steel, but you want it to join a curved piece of steel. How do you do it?

Decide which side you want to bend. One side will bend and the other will stay flat. Place the side you want to bend on an anvil or dolly and start to strike it with a flat hammer. You will need lots of repeated blows with the hammer to get it to spread − for that is what you are doing. You are spreading one side of the steel. The more you strike it, the more it will spread − and the more it spreads, the more it bends. It might sound complicated in words, but have a look at the photographs then try it on a piece of scrap steel. It's quite easy to do. Don't strike too hard or too long, otherwise the steel will get very thin as it spreads. Once you have hammered the steel into the shape you need, you can trim the edge of the hammered side with tin snips or some similar tool.

Basic Bending

If you need to bend a flat sheet of steel to form a ring, how do you do it? The quickest way is to cut out some 'V's and pull the edges of the 'V's together with weld. Try this quick experiment. Take a flat piece of steel about 6 inches long and two inches wide. You want to curve the surface of the steel so that it forms a flat semi-circle. The exact measurements don't matter for this test. Get your tin snips and cut half a dozen 'V' shapes in one long edge of the steel. They need to go almost through to the other edge. But don't cut right through!

The 'V's can be narrow or wide, depending on the amount of bend you need. I suggest narrow ones till you get the idea. When you have cut your 'V's, gently grasp both ends of the steel and try to form a horse-shoe shape. The steel should bend so that the edges of the 'V's close up. If you have done it right, you should have an approximate semi-circle. Try the experiment again with different or more 'V's. You can weld up the 'V's to create a curved piece of steel if you need to.

Instead of a flat shape you might want one with a right angled side. Its exactly the same formula. This time cut the 'V's in the flat edge through to the vertical edge. When you form your horse-shoe you will bend the vertical edge in a nice curve.

The other way get a flat curve is to simply mark out the shape you want on the sur-

Lay the edge you want to bend on the anvil or dolly and strike it with a hammer.

The edge struck with the hammer is uppermost. The hammered edge has expanded and curved the other edge.

Using 'V's to bend metal. In this picture I have only cut one side of the 'V'. Having got the curve right, I can now mark the other side of the 'V' and cut it out.

face of a steel sheet, then cut it out. By careful cutting with tin snips you can get quite intricate shapes. Try it!

Now you have made a 90 degree bend, and a curve – what next. How do you bend a flat sheet into a curve, the sort you find on a rear skirt or valance? If the job requires a long piece of steel, you might have problems coaxing it into shape, but if it is only a few inches long, such as a repair patch, then there is no problem. The best way is to put it through a wheeling machine, but you are not likely to have one of these machines in your workshop, so what alternative is there?

Look for any handy object which is curved. Examples are, your own knee, the wheel on your car, the curved faces on a shoemaker's last, a telephone pole or log, a round street lamp pole etc. Are you getting the idea? I have an old steel wheel which came off some sort of four-wheeled barrow. Its ideal for holding in a vice and shaping metal on. All you need to do is bend the steel round the object which has a shape closest to the one you want to create.

Place the piece of steel to be shaped so that it forms a tangent with the rim of the wheel. If your geometry is like mine, have a look at the photograph, which as usual is worth a thousand words. You want about an inch (or less) of the steel 'hanging' out from the wheel. Now, using a slapper (fully described in the next Chapter) or a hammer or a mallet, tap the steel so that it bends towards the wheel. By gently moving the steel and tapping with the hammer, you will be able to bend the steel to the shape or circumference of the wheel. If you have a job about a foot long, you will have to do a bit at a time, then move the steel along the wheel and repeat the process. The photographs show the technique.

Top Hat

Many of the shapes you will find under a car, making up the chassis, are known as 'top hat' and if you look at the photograph you will see why. The end view of the channel section has a shape like a top hat.

Preparing to form a curve. Place the steel so that about an inch overhangs the curved surface....

...then strike the steel with a mallet or hammer. The steel will bend and follow the curve of the wheel. You may have to move the steel around on the wheel to get the result you want. A different radius will give you a different curve.

The basic building-block of a modern chassis. This 'Top Hat' section has been shaped to form an outrigger. You could make this easily.

Car manufacturers often use this basic shape for their chassis members. Without going into it too deeply, it is light, strong and cheap to make. And, when you add a fourth side you have a very strong assembly.

Mostly this type of section is straight, or nearly straight, but occasionally it can be made with curves in it. I'm thinking here of the chassis section which might run over the rear axle. It starts near the front of the leaf spring, and ends right at the back of the car, fixed to the rear skirt and bumper-bar brackets. This section is almost always curved, to allow the shock-absorber to run up to its top mounting. If you had to try to repair this section you could find it very difficult to copy.

There is an easier way. If you have to patch one side of a top hat section which is curved, you will not be able to curve the side and still have a 90 degree lip. Make the repair patch in two pieces. There is a separate Chapter about Sectioning and Patching, but I want you to tell you about this now as it ties in well with our earlier discussions about 'shape.'

Cut out the piece of steel which will form the side of the top hat section. Make sure you get the curvature exactly right, because in the next step you are going to 'lock' that shape into the steel.

When you have the curved patch cut out, stand it vertically on a piece of card, so that the curved edge is against the card. Now trace the shape by running a pencil along the edge of the steel and the card. You should now have a line on the paper which matches the curves on your patch.

Now, draw another line, EXACTLY the same as the first one, but half an inch apart. You now have the shape of the lip for your patch panel. Cut it out of the steel.

Put the steel in a vice, but DO NOT tighten it up so that you lose the curvature. Making sure that the curved lip is the right way up, weld it carefully along the edge of the patch panel. In this way you have made up a complete patch panel with a half inch lip which really matches the contours of the chassis.

Templates

As I mentioned earlier, you will have to mark out where to bend or cut a piece of steel to make the repair patch or panel you need. This process is helped by a template. A template is simply a piece of paper, card or thin steel which has been made to a certain shape, so that a copy can be made from it.

Templates are so handy and so easy to make that they are often ignored in the

Basic 'Top Hat' shapes again. Different sizes are used to form a chassis. They can be bought from specialist Motor Factors quite cheaply.

'Top Hat' shown as a chassis-member with a piece of ply-wood representing a floor section.

enthusiastic rush to get the job finished. They offer a means of getting a patch panel EXACTLY right, and if you need to use the same type of patch again, you can make a template from a piece of alloy or light steel.

Basically, you need four items to make templates. Sheets of brown wrapping paper, a sheet of card, a pair of scissors and

a sharp pencil. You don't have to buy special card. I have used cornflake packets, the bit of card that is packed with a new shirt and so on. Similarly the paper can be almost anything except newspaper. Why not newspaper? Well it's got printing on, so that makes it harder to see your markings and it's also easily torn. Brown paper, the type used to wrap parcels, is ideal.

Right, let's make a template. Nothing too difficult to start with. Just an unusual, but flat, shape. Lay the piece of paper over the old panel which is to be replaced. Using your fingers, make a crease on the paper along the edges of the panel. Alternatively, lay the panel on top of the paper and draw round it with the pencil. Either way can be used, and there are situations when only one or the other can be used.

When you have the outline right, cut out the shape with the scissors. Offer the paper shape to the metal panel. If it is not an accurate copy, throw away the paper and start again! Don't be discouraged if you have to throw away two or three attempts at the shape. After 20 years I still need a couple of attempts to get it right!

Holes can make for big problems. If your piece of steel needs to have a hole in it, you must get this hole exactly right on the template. If you don't you are wasting your time making the template. If the hole is wrongly located on the template it will also be wrong on the finished job.

I have spent many unhappy hours trying to get holes in the right places. Try these hints. If possible, stick a pencil through the hole, so that a mark is made on the paper. Often this is not possible, so try rubbing your finger over the paper, so that the edges of the hole make a crease in the paper. You may have to find another way yourself, depending on the complexity of the job. However you do it, you MUST get holes exactly located, otherwise the job is spoilt.

When you get it exactly right, transfer the shape onto the card. You can of course go straight from steel to card, but I prefer to use paper so that I get a better 'feel' for the shape being made. As I said just now, I also make a lot of mistakes, so it usually takes me a few attempts to get the shape right!

Once the shape is on steel, cut out the steel with tin snips. If you need to use the template again, why not transfer the template onto a sheet of tin or similar. Cardboard templates could go soggy if you keep them in a damp garage and you would have to go through the process of making another one.

Marking Out

There are several methods of making marks on steel, prior to cutting out. You can use a pencil, or a sharp edge such as a scriber, or simply a sharpened screwdriver. Either way, you will need a good steel rule, and if you can afford it some sort of set-square for marking out right angles. If you need to mark out steel which will be bent, make some sort of mark which you will recognise as a bend mark. It's very important to remember that what you mark out may be 'handed'. That means if

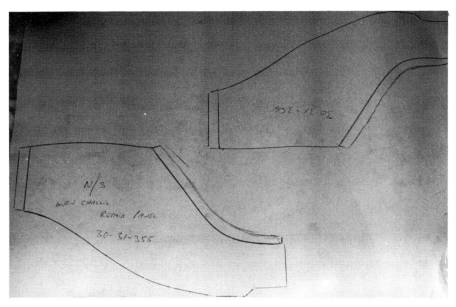

I marked out this 'same size' template for a chassis repair section which I bought. If they ever go out of stock, I can make one from the template.

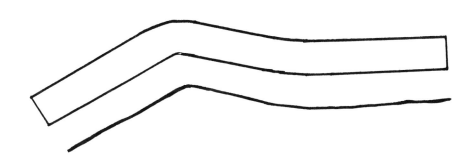

How to make a lip on a curved section. The line is the mark from the edge of the patch, while the lip is developed from the line. Once cut out, the lip is welded on.

you turn the template, or the piece of steel through 180 degrees, it will not fit the position you intended it to go. Think about it. A left-hand glove will not fit a right hand. Even if you turn it over, it is still not correct. Don't get caught out like this. I have occasionally wasted hours making some part only to find I got it upside down or round the wrong way. The simple way to keep things right is mark TOP or OUT or some similar note on the template and on the steel. That way, you are less likely to make an error.

Once again, spend enough time getting any holes in exactly the right position before you cut them out. Even a quarter of an inch can mean you have to start all over again.

The main thing to remember is that accuracy is something that accumulates. If you mark out the steel accurately, it helps you to cut out accurately. And if you cut out accurately the finished job will be more accurate and more difficult to see. As I said earlier, 'You can patch, repair or re-

place, but the neater the job, the greater the satisfaction.'

Now that I have given you a brief insight into what you can do with simple tools and equipment, I want to spend some time describing a number of bodywork tools in the next chapter. There are many, more expensive tools available, but don't let that put you off. I have lots of 'special' tools, but most of the time I use a few favourites which need not cost you a lot. In Chapter Three you'll find lots more tips and techniques to get to grips with.

Panel Craft Tools

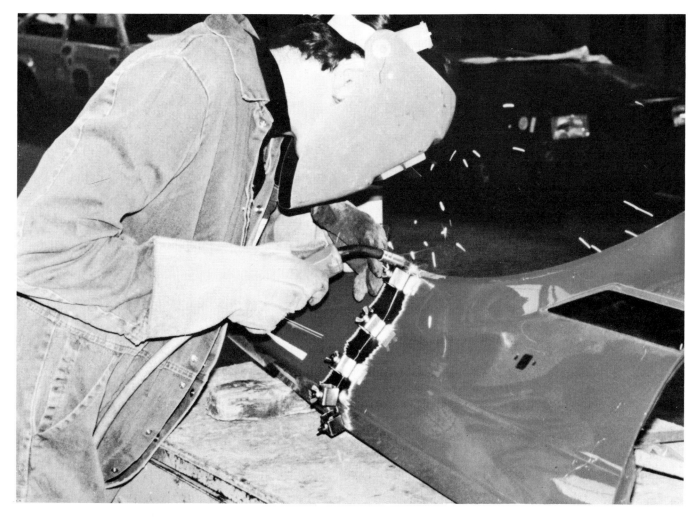

Two pieces of a wing are held together with Inter-grip welding clamps while the welder makes tack welds. When the tacks are in place, the clamps must be removed and a seam weld run along the join.

Panel Craft can be as cheap or as expensive as your pocket will allow. You can achieve excellent results with just a few basic tools which can be added to later as and when you need them.

A very basic tool kit would have to include:

1) A welding set (I prefer gas)

2) Hammer

3) Dolly

4) Wire brush

5) Tin Snips

6) Pair of 'G' clamps

I have to admit that I would find it difficult to manage without some additional tools, but if nothing else was available or money was very tight, then it could be done.

Later on, you can add items like special clamps, high speed angle grinder and so on. In this chapter I want to examine each tool in turn, assess its usefulness and explain briefly how to use it. They are not arranged in any particular order.

Hammers

There are many special hammers on the market today. Each hammer is designed for a particular job and most will last a lifetime if they are looked after. I use four different hammers and they came from widely different sources. Each hammer has a different 'feel' to it, and you get used to a particular hammer after a time. That is why I tend to use an old, beat-up, second-hand hammer rather than a super new professional panel beater's hammer.

First I have a Sykes-Pickavant hammer which I use for dressing edges and general panel work which might be visible (that is, usually on the outside of the bodywork). This hammer has two flat faces, one round and the other square. The square face allows you to get into the corners of right-angled bends, where only a small part of the round face would be useful. (We will discuss terms like 'dressing edges' in a later section).

My second hammer, which I use most of the time is a joiner's staple or pin hammer. I got mine second-hand from an autojumble, but they are widely available and quite cheap. I use this for all sorts of work, including hammering welds.

The third hammer is, I'm told, from the bricklaying trade. It is shown in the photographs and is easily identified by the large spike. This spike can be dangerous, so take care if you decide to use one. I use mine for tapping panels into position, because the spike allows the hammer blow to be directed into inaccessible positions. If you can only afford one hammer, I would advise you to buy this type. Be careful with that spike though!

The last hammer in my collection is a heavy, two-pound hammer. This is used with a four-inch chisel to remove metalwork from car bodies and chassis frames. Two pounds is about as heavy as you want to hold when lying under a car and it does a good job of removal providing the chisel is kept sharp. You may think it a rather rough and ready combination, and you'd be right. But if you want to remove rusty steel, it's no use fussing around. Get it off as quickly and easily as possible.

Pop Rivets

Pop Rivets (sometimes known as lazy rivets) are often overlooked as a method of temporary fixing. They are widely used in the aircraft industry and in building some buses and coaches. They are very cheap, but you do need the pop rivet tool which can be expensive. If you decide to use pop rivets as a fastener prior to welding, use washers to sandwich the steel panels together while doing up the rivet. This is a job that really needs three hands, so ask for a volunteer before you start.

Once you have welded the new panels into position, you can either melt the rivet away (which can be a bit messy, leaving bits of aluminium around) or you can just grind off the head and the rivet will fall out. Fill in the holes by 'Blobbing' as described in a later Chapter.

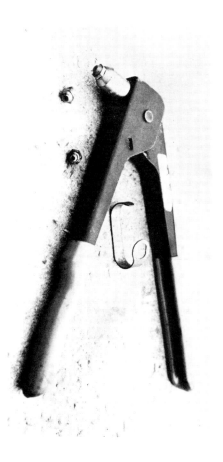

The pop rivet gun. This one has a choice of three heads, which will take different sized rivets.

One of an extensive range of professional-quality hammers available from Sykes-Pickavant, this hammer has a round face and a square face.

Clamps

I want to split this section into two halves. The first deals with our old friend the 'G' clamp, sometimes known as a 'C' clamp. The second section looks at more specialised clamps designed for welders.

'G' Clamps

'G' clamps are so well known that I will just refer you to the photographs rather than describe them. The idea is that they clamp two or more pieces of material together between two jaws, one of which is on a screw thread. They are best with overlapped material, and not very useful for butt joints. You will need to include a couple of 'G' clamps in your welder's toolbox because they have so many different uses. You need them in various sizes, but small ones, capable of clamping material an inch thick, will make an ideal start to your collection.

The heavy hammer. I use this one with a chisel to remove unwanted steel from chassis sections. It weighs two pounds.

This hammer is useful for tapping awkward chassis sections into place during welding. I think it is intended for brick-layers.

Welding Clamps

Numerous welding clamps are available and you should start saving for some now, or else drop big hints near birthday time. I have about five or six pairs including what I think are the best ones. They are from the makers of Mole clamps and have four-inch wide blades. This allows them to clamp a nice wide area which makes for a secure job. Their only drawback is the wide jaw, which may be too wide to cope with curves, or to fit into confined spaces. Once you have a pair of these, you will wonder how you ever managed before. (By the way, when I say a pair — I mean one, just like in 'a pair of pliers'.)

These clamps will hold butt or overlap joints and will cover a variety of thicknesses.

I find that these clamps sometimes tend to release due to vibration, such as when dressing a weld with a hammer; or you set up a job with all the clamps in place and decide a slight adjustment is needed. A tap with a hammer to move a panel and the whole lot gives way as the clamp opens. Now, it may be just a fault on my clamps, which have seen a lot of use, but bear it in mind and if it happens to you it won't come as a total surprise. Make sure you do up the clamp as tight as possible.

Several clamps are shown in the photographs, but remember you get what you pay for and the quality of these clamps varies enormously. Buy the best. Keep your eyes open in local junk shops or visit the nearest autojumble or swap meet.

Mole Clamps

The traditional Mole clamp will give good results although you are somewhat limited by the narrow jaws.

When you try to clamp two pieces of steel together in a butt joint there can be problems, especially if the jaws are narrow. To solve this problem various other types of clamp have been devised. Some are expensive for what they are, but all are very useful and at times indispensable for particular jobs.

Wedgelock-type Fasteners

Let's look at a nice cheap alternative first. I discovered these clamps in an American metalworking book. I later discovered that they cost around £2 each. Being mean, I thought that was too much to pay, especially when you needed to buy a special set of pliers to operate the clamp. The pliers cost about £7. Then I happened to visit an autojumble which had some aircraft parts for sale. There were boxes and boxes of *similar* clamps – priced at just one penny each. I bought a lot! They are widely used in the aircraft industry to hold sheets of alloy onto airframes prior to rivetting. Their beauty is that they are screw-adjustable, so don't need any special tools.

Another advantage is that they can be adjusted to clamp quite a large range of thicknesses and if you use two washers to increase the clamping area, they can be used to hold a butt-joint. The only snag is the thickness of the clamping wire means that the gap between the two panels being held is a little large.

Inter-grip Clamps

The next alternative cures the above problem but is more expensive. They are called Inter-grip welding clamps and come in packs of four or five. Halfords sell them in the UK or you can contact the manufacturer whose address is given at the end of the book. They provide a nice tight clamping action, but I find they are sometimes a little tricky to fit. The screw could be made just a little longer which would aid the fitting process. However, I have been using a set for about a year now and would recommend them.

Nuts and Bolts

There is an even cheaper way to hold two

The "C" clamp, otherwise known as the "G" clamp. Either way, you need a few in your toolbox.

A choice of welding clamps. The one in the middle, with the four-inch wide jaws is probably the most useful. I use two of them all the time.

pieces of steel together. Get yourself a handful of BA sized nuts, bolts and washers. These are the sort of fasteners which you buy in little plastic packets from Do It Yourself shops. You can get three nuts and bolts for about twenty pence. Get the ones where the underside of the head is flat, rather than the tapered, countersunk ones. This makes for easier fitting.

You can sandwich the panel steel between the washers while you tighten up the bolts. This method is quite good enough if you are on a tight budget, and I sometimes use it for certain jobs.

Edge Setter

There are many ways to set a 90 degree edge or lip on a piece of steel, but perhaps the simplest way took me the longest to discover. You can make the simple little tool which does this job for free as follows:

Get hold of a piece of hexagonal or square bar (I use an old chisel with the cutting end removed). This leaves you with just the hexagon handle. Now get a hacksaw and fit TWO steel-cutting blades together in the hacksaw. Put the hexagon bar vertically in a vice with the 'cut' end upwards. Now cut a vertical slot in the bar. Make the slot as straight as you can and as deep as the hacksaw blade. Remove from the vice, smooth off any rough edges with a file and there you have it — an edge setter. Have a look at the photographs to see the finished article.

To set an edge, put the slot over the edge of a piece of steel and rotate the tool through 90 degrees. You will find that the steel will not bend a full 90 degrees. Move the tool along about an inch and repeat the bend. As you move along the steel a lip will form. Once you have done as much as you can with the edge setter, get out your hammer and a dolly with a straight edge and finish the job. Again, there is a photograph to show this.

You can also make edges with a pair of pliers, or your welding clamps, or just with the hammer and dolly, but this simple little tool makes it much easier and neater, since you always get an edge the same size. You may be able to think up some improvements to this basic tool, but I recommend you make one as soon as you start any serious panel work.

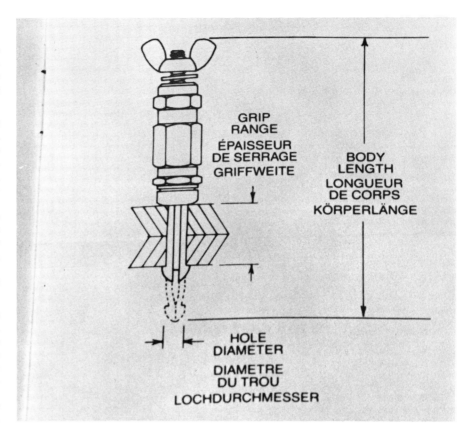

How the Wedgelock clamp works. Two steel wires are pushed through the hole, and when the device is tightened, the wires exert a strong pull on the steel. (Courtesy A.T.A. Engineering Processes).

Tank Cutters

Tank cutters are devices which cut large diameter holes in sheet metal. There are two types. The first type consists of a circular blade which has a pilot drill in the middle. You start to drill using the pilot drill, and once the pilot has established the hole, the circular cutter starts to cut the

A Wedgelock type fastener holds the top of this sill in position. This is one of a lot I bought at an autojumble. They needed to be cleaned in petrol before they could be used, but I find they are very useful. These are tough little tools which provide a strong clamping action.

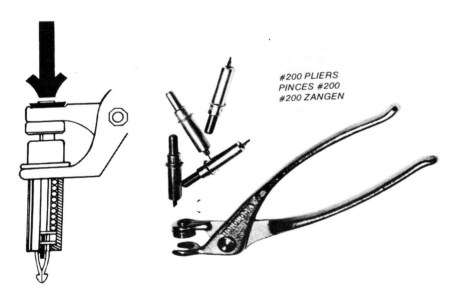

#200 PLIERS
PINCES #200
#200 ZANGEN

Another type of Wedgelock clamp is operated by special pliers. These are really handy if you are fabricating panels or repair sections from sheet metal. (Courtesy A.T.A. Engineering Processes).

Get hold of an old chisel. This one has a broken end and had been thrown away.

Cut the end off the chisel to make the handle for your edge setting tool.

The edge setter. A simple device which you will use all the time. You may be able to improve on this basic design!

steel. This type of cutter needs a very slow cutting speed, otherwise the blade overheats and quickly becomes blunt.

The second type consists of a pilot drill which has an arm extending from it. on the end of the arm is another cutting edge. This arm usually has some sort of adjustment so that you can make the hole to the required size. Again, it needs a slow cutting speed. Both these types of cutter are best with a hand-drill. They are used for larger diameter holes, such as 1-1/2' and upwards. For smaller holes use a chassis punch.

Chassis Punches

The chassis punch is a neat device used in the days when radios still had tubes. The tubes had to be mounted in holders, and the holders needed a hole in the metal chassis. The chassis punch consists of a circular anvil and circular cutting edge. The two are brought together by a screw tightened by an Allen key. As you tighten the screw the cutting edge bites through

the steel which is supported by the anvil underneath. You can get them in all sorts of sizes, Imperial and metric, but they will only cut the size you buy. There is no adjustment.

Drill a pilot hole where you want the larger hole to be. Then put the driving screw through the hole with the cutter above. Thread on the anvil part and start to tighten. You need an Allen key to drive the screw. They make really neat, clean cuts.

You might like to buy one which cuts a hole the size of the drain holes in your floor panels. When you buy a chassis punch, buy a stock of rubber grommets the same size.

Electric Drill

This is your old friend the electric power drill. It will drive a variety of attachments, including drills, grinding stones and several kinds of rotating wire brushes. It would be very difficult to do any serious

work without access to a power drill, but again you might be able to buy one second hand. I got a new Black and Decker on special offer for £15. I use it mostly for drilling and wire brushing as I am lucky enough to have the next tool on the list, the angle grinder.

Angle Grinder

If ever a tool scared me half to death its the angle grinder! It needs constant care during use, as the grinding material rotates at about 10,000 RPM which is FAST. It is a very effective tool for removing rust and grinding down welds. Depending on the grade (or coarseness) of the sanding discs you can get a very smooth finish very quickly.

A few more words about the angle grinder. *WEAR GOGGLES* and protective clothing when using it. Don't leave it lying around unattended, as a child could be seriously injured. Its got quite a kick as it starts up. Bits fly about so fast, you can do permanent damage to yourself and the car before you realize what is happening.

The chassis punch is available for a few pounds and cuts really neat holes in metalwork. As long as you keep it clean and greased it will last a long time.

Be very careful selecting attachments for this tool, as wire brushes have to be specially made to rotate at the high speed of this tool. I once used the wrong type of wire cup brush when removing rust from the underside of a car. The brush almost disintegrated in about five minutes due to the high speed. This was bad enough, but for the next year little pieces of wire kept appearing in the car, in the driveway, and in my overalls!

I've also had a sanding disc break up on me, as it snagged on a bit of ragged metal. The disc fragmented and flew in all directions. One piece cut me across the back of the hand, leaving a wound which has a one inch scar. I should have been wearing gloves − make sure you do.

The smallest angle grinder can be bought from about £40 upwards. Sanding discs vary in price depending on quality and coarseness. Typically, you might get two for £1.

Let me end the discussion on the angle grinder with another warning. The little sparks given off when grinding are particularly nasty. They seem to travel faster than the starship Enterprise and can inflict the same amount of damage as a photon torpedo! *DON'T LET THE SPARKS HIT ANY WINDSHIELD OR GLASS.* The sparks embed themselves in glass, and you can imagine what this will do to a set of windscreen wiper rubbers. If you don't take care over this, you will cost yourself a lot of money.

Verdict − very useful, but potentially very dangerous! Wear goggles, gloves and other protection.

Metal Folder

This is not the sort of tool the home panel man is going to have lying around. They can be bought from £300 upwards, but you will probably get your local sheet-metal shop to bend any special shapes you want on their machine. It will be well worthwhile asking the operator what can be done on these machines, as they are very versatile and are not restricted to straight line bends. I have had some beautiful sills made up by a skilled man using a metal folder. They were cheap too!

If you have a friend in the sheet-metal trade, its worth the price of a couple of beers to find out what these machines can do. You never know when you might need work done on one.

Wheeling Machine

I want to spend a little time looking at this device. Its not likely that you will have one in your home workshop, they cost from £300 upwards (second-hand) and are big heavy machines. They were widely used in

Our old friend the electric drill. This one was on special offer and cost about £15. The wire brush is going a bit bald, though!

The high speed angle grinder makes quick work of grinding down welds, but needs to be handled carefully.

the good old days, when cars were cars and men were skilled craftsmen who could be given a flat sheet of steel and produce a beautifully sculptured wing.

The basic theory is that you pass a flat sheet of steel through the two rollers, which can be adjusted to vary the pressure between them. This pressure, together with the radius of the rollers will tend to curve the steel. Using a lot of skill, a good craftsman can make all sorts of interesting

shapes on the Wheeling machine.

If you ever come across one of these at a knock-down price let me know!

Mallet

Once again, I did not have a mallet for years and years, until I found one in a jumble sale for 50 pence. They are useful for certain jobs, where it is important NOT to mark the face of the steel. They are also used a lot in the 'Hot Shrinking' process which is described in the next Chapter. Not a 'must-have' tool, but a useful addition.

Joddler

This strange device puts a 'step' in the edge of a flat panel. The idea is that the step is the same thickness as the steel panel, so another piece of steel panel will lie in the step to provide a smooth join. My tool cost about £25 and I don't use it very much. Nowadays I prefer to weld steel with butt joints, so the Joddler (also knows as a Joggler) lies in my toolbox, idle much of the time. I think it depends on your welding skill if you buy one or not. Many people say the joggle joint is easier for the amateur to manage.

With this tool, I recommend you try before you buy.

The head of the Joddler or Joggler. The device on the left creates the step, while on this example another device on the right punches a small hole.

Dolly

There are dozens of dollies available from the specialised suppliers, and Halfords usually have a few to choose from. Sykes-Pickavant have over a dozen in their catalogue, so you should be able to find one suitable for every job.

The dolly is simply an anvil. A piece of steel is supported by the anvil, while it is hammered. It sounds very simple, but hammer and dolly work is a skill which takes a long time to master.

I use one favourite dolly most of the time. It is known as a Toe Dolly. Don't ask me why, but it is to do with the shape! I have a few other dollies which I have bought over the years and I use them occasionally.

I suppose you will laugh, but the best way to treat a dolly, which is a precision-ground, hardened tool, is to keep it in an oily sock.

Dollies galore. They are: 547 Angle dolly, 548 Thin Toe, 550 Grid, 549 General Purpose, 551 Double End, 552 Utility, 553 Curved, 554 Heel, 555 Anvil, 556 Dome, 557 Round, 558 Toe, 559 Shrinking, 543 Lightweight Curved, 534 Heel. (Courtesy Sykes-Pickavant Ltd).

My favourite dolly, known as a "Toe Dolly". I got this one second-hand and I use it all the time.

The simple wooden mallet. This one cost just 50 pence from a jumble sale.

I am making this dolly from an old railway tie-bar. It can be mounted in a vice and used as a simple anvil.

A selection of home-made dollies and devices. They all have a use and didn't cost much. Why not try making some yourself?

Shrinking Dolly

I have singled this dolly out for a special mention as it can be very useful if you are joining a lot of pieces of steel, such as when patching a panel. The shrinking dolly has a groove down one face, into which you can hammer a line of weld. This tightens the panel and resists any distortion in the sheet. See Hammer Welding in the next Chapter.

Another type of shrinking dolly is the Grid Dolly. This has a raised pattern on one face and is used to cold-shrink a panel. I have never used one, but the theory is that the steel is shaped over the little raised lumps and tends to reduce in surface area.

Home Made Dollies

As you become more experienced in shaping metal you will probably acquire a few more dollies. I have four purpose-made professional dollies. Then I realised that I have a lot more. I use round tubes, wheels, a piece of railway line, bits of angle iron and so on. So the answer is buy one dolly, then make your own.

One dolly which I am currently making is cut from an old railway tie-bar or fishplate. That is the big plate which is used to bolt two lengths of railway line together. When I was digging out a pit in my garage, I found one in the foundations. It took about half an hour's solid cutting with a hacksaw to cut a piece off, but I spread this effort over about four evenings, so it wasn't too painful.

The unfinished dolly is shown in the photograph. I intend to smooth off the edge of

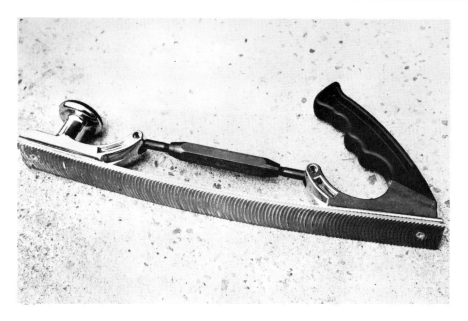

This body file has an adjusting device which allows the blade to be convex or concave. That way, it can be used on all sorts of different curved surfaces.

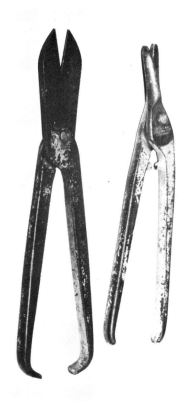

Choice of two tin snips. The top ones have cranked handles while the lower ones have straight handles.

the hole, so that I can use it for different jobs, such as making a groove or taking the stretch out of a big flat panel. It needs more work to get it right, but I hope it gives you an idea to make your own dolly.

Screwdriver or Scriber

A simple one, this. Get an old screwdriver (a small one) and grind the end to a point. Now you have a tool for scratching lines on sheet steel. You could always buy a special scriber in the Toolstore, but the cheap alternative is good enough.

Slapper

This device can be simple or expensive. I use the simple, cheap alternative. Get yourself a flat tyre-iron (tyre lever) about a foot long. Now use it instead of using a hammer. Do I need to point out that you use the flat face, not the edge? This is a useful tool for dressing edges as it does not leave marks on the steel which you might

do if you use the hammer a bit too hard. It's a nice cheap tool that I like to keep handy. You can buy expensive ones with nice shaped handles, but I think I'll stick to my basic tyre lever.

Another variation on the above is to get an old file and bend it using the welding torch as a heat source. Bend it like a Z — shape so that you have a handle. Use this to shrink steel panels which have been heated. Metal shrinking is described in another Chapter.

Bodyfile

There are several types of bodyfile available, but the one in the photograph is the type which is adjustable. You turn the turnbuckle in the middle and one way makes the surface of the file convex, the other way and it becomes concave. In this manner you adjust the tool to match closely the contour of the panel being filed.

This type of file is very useful for removing excess plastic filler, giving a quick smooth action. The other use of the body file is to file a series of marks in one direction across a panel, then another series of marks at right angles to the first. If you have any low spots on the panel they will show up by not being shiny. (That is, being below the level of the rest of the panel, they will not be reached by the file). This gives a good indication of where more hammer and dolly work might be needed.

Many different blades are available for the body file. UK readers should have a look in the Sykes-Pickavant catalogue for a

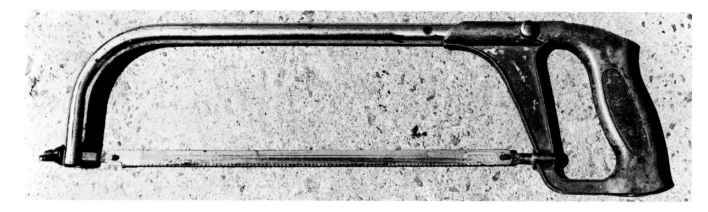

Our old friend the hacksaw. This tool is a must for the toolbox, as is a selection of top-quality blades for cutting steel. Don't mess around with cheap blades, as they are not worth the trouble.

selection of blades. Overseas readers will have to ask at their tool store.

Dent Puller

This tool is favoured by many panel beaters. It consists of a handle, a shaft, a hook or self-tapping screw at one end and a sliding weight. You screw the self-tapping screw into the steel panel in a low spot, then hold the handle with one hand, and jerk the weight along the shaft. The weight multiplied by the speed at which it is jerked, causes the self-tapping screw to pull the low spot out. That's the theory. I've never had too much success with this, but you might have more luck. The slide-hammer is very useful if it saves you a lot of dismantling work, for example where a panel has a lot of interior trim attached.

Suction Cup

Big suction cups, (often known as 'Suckers') can be applied to a large flat area of steel, and often prove useful in pulling out big shallow dents. However, big shallow dents might pop back in just as quickly!

Tin Snips

You must buy a good set of tin snips. There are many lengths of handle generally available depending on the type of snips. Some types have straight handles, while others have cranked handles. I prefer the cranked-handle type. Once you have decided straight or cranked, and the length, you need to specify right handed or left handed. No, it's not to do with being right or left-handed. It refers to which side the waste steel should come off when cutting. Think about cutting along a curved line. Right hand snips remove metal from the right of the marked line. Left hand

You MUST wear goggles when using abrasive tools such as the electric drill or angle grinder. These are readily available and could save you from serious injury. Wear them.

snips remove metal from the left of the line. So if you were trimming along the right hand edge of a flat piece of steel, you would want right hand snips to remove a right hand ragged edge. The design of the snip jaws helps to move the scrap metal to one side to make for an easier cut. Try it if you have the chance. You can get by with just one set of snips.

Choose snips from a top quality maker and be prepared to pay a lot for them, say from £15 upwards. They will be worth it, as you will use them every time you do metalwork on your car. Choose a set that are comfortable in your hands, otherwise you will get blisters. (You'll probably get blisters anyway, if you are not accustomed to using snips!)

Hacksaw

Everyone knows the common hacksaw. But did you know about choosing the correct blade? There are different blades for different materials, so make sure you get one suitable for mild steel. It is no use trying to cut steel with a blade designed for cutting wood. If you are in doubt, ask at the Tool Store.

Junior Hacksaw

This is the little wire-framed version of the hacksaw. It's a very useful tool, and blades are very cheap when you buy them in packets of ten or twenty. I'd recommend you have one of these. They are great for cutting off small corners when fitting chassis or frame repair sections. They are also ideal when you have to make your own repair section.

Screw Jack

I've included this as it is useful for holding repair sections and floor sections in position prior to welding. It is often overlooked when you are searching for a means of temporary fixing.

Chisel

No doubts here. You need a four-inch, flat, cold-chisel. They are readily available

Abrasive discs for the angle grinder. These are available in many different "grits", which means the size of the abrasive grit on the paper. The lower the grit number, the rougher the disc. These are 80 grit.

in tool stores and make quick work of dismantling spot welds. Keep the blade sharp and in good condition. The sharper the blade the easier the cut, and the less the two panels will suffer in the process.

Zipcut Spot-Weld Tool

This is a Sykes-Pickavant tool which is used with a slow-turning drill, maximum speed 900 rpm, to cut through spot welds.

I have never used one, but they may be the answer to your particular problem. The blade can be adjusted for depth of cut and both ends of the blade can be used.

Inspection Lamp

I have two types of inspection lamp. The first type is the most popular, being designed to plug into the mains. Make sure your power lead is safe (not cut or damaged) and don't run the wire through puddles.

My second inspection lamp is the type you plug into the cigar lighter on the car dashboard. They only cost a couple of pounds and use a sidelight bulb. They are quite useful for getting into tight corners, being much more compact than the mains type. There are some with a magnetic base, so you can stick them in exactly the right place. The only drawback is that if you are restoring a car, you will have removed the battery long ago. Worth considering for the toolbox, though.

Inspection Pit

An inspection pit is really great for getting under cars. However, it has many disadvantages, so hang on just a second before reaching for your pick and shovel.

Once you are under the car, in the pit, welding, who is up above looking out for fire? You must work with a buddy or

The junior hacksaw in action. You must have one of these in your tool box. They are so cheap and so useful you can't really afford to be without one!

helper when using a pit.

Also, if you are like me and have to build your pit in a small lock-up garage, how do you get under the car once it's over the pit? Access to and from the pit can be difficult, especially if it's 20-below outside and you want to shut the door.

Finally, it might flood in times of high rainfall.

Ideally the pit should be about six feet long, three feet wide and roughly shoulder height deep.

Axle Stands

The poor man's pit? Well not really! You have probably seen axle stands in the accessory shops. Buy a good quality set, because it's your head they are protecting. Normally axle stands have some sort of adjustment to vary their extended height. This may be a pin which you insert into a

The Ford Cortina jack being used to hold a new outrigger in position during a trial fitting.

This rubber sanding block is really good for holding abrasive paper. It costs a couple of pounds, but helps to save your knuckles. You get a better finish using a block.

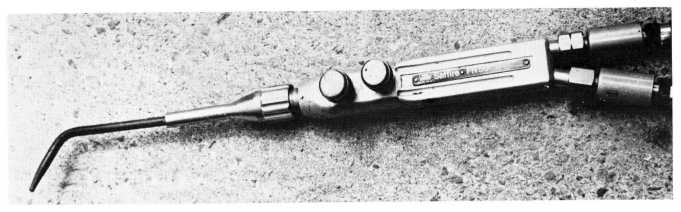

The single most useful tool invented for car body restoration — the gas welding torch. This Saffire torch from BOC can take different tips, and can be fitted with a cutting attachment too.

hole in the stem. Make sure the pin is properly inserted before working under the car.

RAMPS

These are useful for gaining a bit of height when you need to work underneath a car. They have an advantage in that you can drive up onto them, but if you are restoring a bodyshell, you might not have an engine! Useful, but I would choose the axle-stands and a decent jack instead.

PULLING POSTS

If you have the use of a lock-up type garage or a fully equipped workshop, have you considered sinking a few 'pulling posts' into the floor?

The idea is this; drill or chip out a hole in the concrete floor about 10 inches deep and big enough to accommodate a scaffold pole. Next, cut off a piece of the pole about 10 inches long. I think there are two types of scaffold pole. One type is made of some sort of cast iron material which is hard to cut, the other is steel tube which can be cut more readily. Cement this tube into place in the hole, so that the top of the scaffold pole is flush with the concrete floor. Now get hold of some solid steel bar, about two or three feet long, big enough to be a neat fit inside the scaffold pole.

This device allows a car to be rolled over to any angle. The picture board shows the sequence of events, and it only takes a few minutes. The equipment costs around £500, so it will be out of the reach of most enthusiasts. Very handy, though!

Equipment like this engine hoist can be hired by the day or the week. Here the author swaps an engine with a hydraulic hoist. It cost about £10 for two days hire.

Now, if you need to pull a wing out you have something to attach your pulling device to. When not needed, remove the solid bar and stand it in the corner. A plastic cover will help to keep debris out of the hole.

In the professional workshop similar holes are located all round the bodyshop, so that various pulling and pushing devices can be used to straighten out a car. Alternatively, a special jig is used which has attaching points for chains and wires.

Now, remember that we are not dealing with major accident damage in this book. But there are many occasions when it could be useful to have a pulling post at each end of the garage. You can use ropes, chains or pulley systems to achieve the required pull.

To attach the pulling device to the car body, use plates welded or brazed on. Just get a length of steel wire, such as a six-inch nail, bend it into a 'U'-shape, and braze the ends to the bodywork. These can be removed after the job is done and the panel finished with a grinder. This has been a very brief description of a major accident technique. If you need to know more, there are a number of books available which describe these methods fully.

I hope I have given you an idea about sheet-metal working tools, and panel beating tools. There are many more devices available, so I suggest you start acquiring catalogues from the manufacturers.

Remember what I said about tools, at the end of Chapter One? 'Most of the time I use a few favourites which need not cost you a lot.' Choose carefully, and try to buy the best.

In the next Chapter I will tell you about gas welding, and lots of know-how gathered in twenty years of amateur metal-working.

Have you considered hiring welding equipment? You could do all the cutting out and preparing, and hire when you are ready. Ask at your local hire shop; look in Yellow Pages!

Tips And Techniques

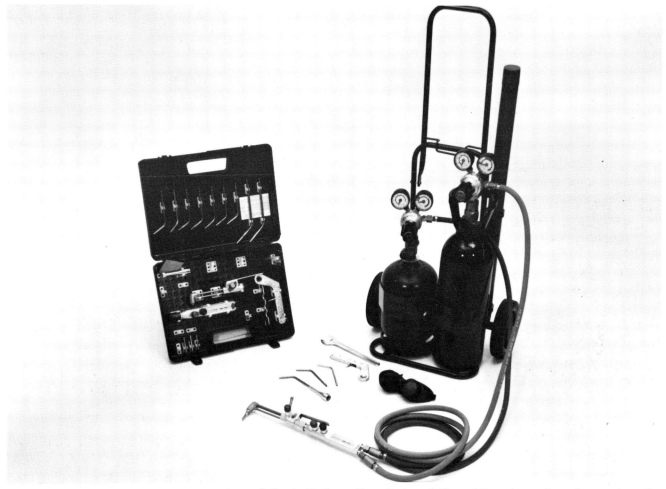

The compact Portapak equipment showing the torch fitted with the cutting attachment. The welding mixer and nozzles are above the cutting torch. The equipment comes in the case on the left.

In this book I only discuss gas welding. And by gas welding I mean welding with oxygen and acetylene. I know there are many other methods of welding now available to the home restorer, but I am not familiar with them, so cannot tell you what to do.

I have found that the gas flame is so completely versatile that I would not be without it. You can do so many things with the gas torch including heat, weld, braze and cut. Try doing some of them with electric arc or the more fashionable argon arc. I don't want you to think I am running these other methods down. Far from it. They are all good methods in the right hands and in the right circumstances, but for complete versatility there is nothing to touch gas.

A few years ago there were difficulties getting supplies of oxygen and acetylene, but these days there is no problem. British Oxygen Company sell a really neat system called PORTAPAK which uses small portable cylinders. I paid about £300 for mine a few years ago and the only thing I've had

to replace are gas and welding rods. The rest of the system, torch, regulators, hoses etc. have never given any trouble.

I am not going to attempt to tell you how to gas weld. There are many books available on the subject which go into it in great detail. Welding is a matter of practice. The more you do, the better and neater you become. I have had a look at some of the welding jobs I did five years ago and compared them with what I can do now. I have definitely improved. Read the section on Gas Welding in the shaded text.

Before we go on, it is worth pausing for a few minutes to define some words you will be reading about. They are all used in welding and you should make yourself familiar with them so that you can make yourself understood if you contract-out some welding.

Torch

The torch is the device that the welder holds in his hand. It consists of a mixing tube which is connected by two hoses to

the tanks of acetylene and oxygen. On the end of the torch is a nozzle or tip, depending on the type of torch. This nozzle or tip can be removed (when the torch is shut down) and exchanged for a larger or smaller tip to suit the work being done.

Filler Rod

This is the material that the welder uses to flow into the two pieces of metal being welded. Filler rod comes in various sizes and is normally flux-coated. The flux allows a better weld to be made.

Gas Cylinder or Tanks

These are the pressure vessels which contain the gas. They are very strong steel tubes, which are regularly pressure-tested by the owners, the company who supplies the gas. In the UK, these cylinders are never sold. They are only rented.

Gas Welding

The following text is reprinted with kind permission from *Gas Control Equipment Limited, Peel Road, West Pimbo, Skelmersdale, Lancs, WN8 9QA.*

Lighting the Blowpipe (Torch)

To ignite the blowpipe, open the fuel-gas control valve and light gas with a spark-lighter. When doing so ensure the spark-lighter is held at right angles to the nozzle.

Adjust the blowpipe valve until the flame just ceases to smoke then gradually turn-on the blowpipe oxygen control valve until the white cone of the flame is sharply defined with the merest trace of acetylene haze. In this condition the flame is neutral and is burning approximately equal volumes of oxygen and acetylene. It is advisable to have slight haze of acetylene around the centre cone, because there is a tendency for the flame to become slightly oxydising as welding proceeds and in most cases it is harmful to the weld to have excess oxygen. See Figure 1.

Shutting down the Blowpipe (Torch)

Shut off acetylene first by closing the blowpipe control valve then follow with closure of the oxygen valve. Close the supply fuel gas valves on the cylinders. Then open and close the blowpipe valves one at a time to relieve pressure in the system – ensuring the gauges register zero – oxygen first then acetylene. Wind back the pressure adjusting screws on both oxygen and acetylene regulators. If the equipment is to be used in the immediate future it is not necessary to close the cylinder valves.

Nozzle (or tip) Maintenance

Do not maltreat a nozzle. Do not use it as a hammer or lever.

To clean nozzle orifices, sets of special nozzle cleaning reamers are available from BOC. Should these not be available use a drill one size smaller than the orifice and work it up and down without twisting; the drill should be held in a pin vice. If the drill does not enter easily start with a smaller drill increasing the size until the correct diameter is attained. Effective flame shape can only be maintained if gas orifices are sharp and square with the end of the nozzle.

If a nozzle becomes damaged on the end, rub it down with a sheet of fine emery laid on a flat surface such as a sheet of glass, taking care to keep the nozzle square with the rubbing surface. The orifice should then be cleaned out as described above. The nozzle has been designed to make this reconditioning possible.

WELDING TECHNIQUES

Leftward Welding

Leftward welding is used on steel for flanged edge welds, for unbevelled plates up to 3.2 mm (1/8') and for bevelled plates up to 5 mm (3/16'). It is also the method usually adopted for cast iron and non-ferrous metals. Welding is started at the right-hand end of the joint and proceeds towards the left.

The blowpipe is given a forward motion with a slight sideways movement to maintain melting of the edges of both plates at the desired rate and the welding rod is moved progressively along the weld seam. See Figure 2.

Figure 1.

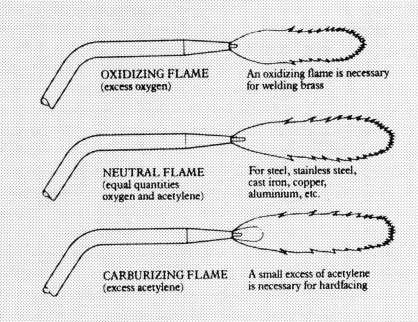

OXIDIZING FLAME (excess oxygen)

An oxidizing flame is necessary for welding brass

NEUTRAL FLAME (equal quantities oxygen and acetylene)

For steel, stainless steel, cast iron, copper, aluminium, etc.

CARBURIZING FLAME (excess acetylene)

A small excess of acetylene is necessary for hardfacing

Figure 2.

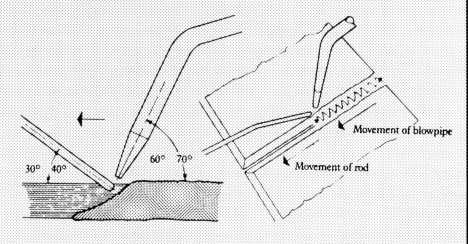

30° 40°   60° 70°   Movement of blowpipe   Movement of rod

The knob controls the gas pressure, while the contents of the cylinder are indicated by the plastic tube on the top.

Regulators

These are the devices mounted on top of the cylinders which control the flow of gas. The gas is stored at very high pressures, but is only required at low pressure at the tip. The regulator adjusts the flow of the gas. Sometimes the same gauge also indicates the amount of gas contained in the cylinders. Some equipment has a little tube with a coloured marker to indicate the level of gas remaining in the tank.

These are the bottles or cylinders which contain the gas. The larger bottle contains oxygen, the smaller acetylene.

Goggles

These are the protective eye-shields worn by welders. The goggles must comply with the latest UK British Standard for safety,

At the top of the bottle is a control valve which allows gas to flow from the cylinder. A key controls the valve.

so ask your dealer when you buy them. You can buy several different types of goggles, including those which will fit over spectacles.

Some other words you need to know refer to the different ways you can join two or more pieces of steel, and if you look at the accompanying drawings you will get the idea.

Butt Weld

A butt weld is made when two (or more) pieces of steel are pushed together, edge on. They literally 'butt' together and are then welded in place. The bits of steel to be butt-welded are usually kept apart a little, to leave a gap for expansion. Into this gap goes the filler rod, and this practice ensures less distortion. When the welding is finished, you have to smooth off the weld with a grinder and finish with a wipe of plastic filler.

Overlap Weld

An overlap weld is made with two pieces of steel, one of which lies on top of the other. The weld is made by melting the edge of one piece of steel into the surface of the other, with the help of some filler rod. This technique is very common but is more prone to distortion than butt-welding. This weld is also finished off with

The Sifbronze Inter-grip is the ideal solution to the problem of holding sheet metal accurately in place and perfectly flush while a butt weld is being made—so minimising all that unnecessary dressing and making good.

Being simple to use and quick to release the Sifbronze Inter-grip will save time on almost every job. Inter-grips are manufactured from zinc plated mild steel.

INSTRUCTIONS

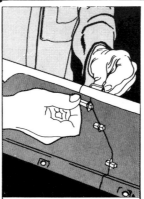

For mid section welding.

Fix first clamp loosely to new section. Offer up roughly in position and tighten Inter-grip.

Apply second clamp by inserting the toggle bar when the spacer is positioned between the sections to be welded.

Finalize position and fully tighten Inter-grips.

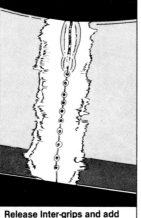

Fit extra Inter-grips at regular intervals. This will ensure flush fitting and will reduce heat distortion problems while tacking.

Tack between Inter-grips. (Do not tack within 10mm of the Inter-grips or withdrawal of spacer can be difficult.)

Release Inter-grips and add tack welds in place of Inter-grips.

Complete weld.

APPLICATIONS Ideal for part panel replacement, mid section welding, clamping curves and awkward shapes.... it's the essential addition to every welder's tool box.

Easily fitted....Quickly released.

a grinder, but by its very nature needs more plastic filler to achieve a neat finish.

Joggle Joint

This unusual name is given to a joint where one piece of steel is stepped, so that the other piece of steel will fit flush to the surface. This is illustrated by the sketch. This technique is also very commonly used, but normally requires a special tool to make the 'Joggle.' You can make the joggle or step with a hammer and dolly, but I have not had a lot of success with this method. This method requires the least finishing, and only a small amount of plastic filler to achieve a smooth finish.

I must admit that I find the joggle joint over-rated. I normally use the butt joint and try to weld more carefully.

Angle Joint

The angle, where two pieces of steel are joined together at an angle, is useful, as you can often melt the two bits of steel into one without using filler rod. I often use this technique.

All these techniques are widely used in the body repairing trades and will be examined in more detail later in the book.

One of the things you don't find in other bodywork books is advice about the size of tip to use in the torch. I have gradually moved towards a smaller tip over the years. I started out with a roaring flame and a number 3 tip, then moved to a

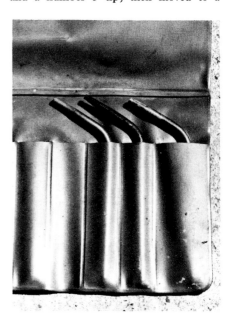

Different size nozzles or tips are stored in this plastic wallet.The smaller tip is a number 1, a larger one being number 5.

This instruction sheet says it all! They can solve a lot of problems, so I recommend you get a set.

quieter flame as I got more confident. Then I tried a number 2 tip and finally a number 1 tip. I occasionally use the number 2 for chassis or frame welding (even going back up to the number 3 on rare occasions) but for all general panel work I use a number 1 tip.

I like to keep a nice low flame, which allows me plenty of control over what I am doing, but I never seem to get it as low as some professional welders.

There are three basic types of gas welding flame. These flames are known as Carbonising, Neutral and Oxidising flames. They are described in the following paragraphs because it is very important that you realise what type of flame you are using.

Before we look at flames just a word of warning. Don't attempt to weld without goggles. You are a fool if you try and an even bigger fool if you blind yourself. Don't do it. You cannot hope to weld properly without goggles.

Carbonising Flame

The carbonising flame (also known as carburising flame or reducing flame) occurs where you have more acetylene than oxygen. The flame is larger and softer and looks yellow when viewed through the goggles. This flame, when used with mild steel produces a fluffy soft looking weld puddle which is carbon-rich and hence weaker than a neutral weld. Carbon tends to harden the mild steel and if it gets too hard it will crack producing dangerous welds.

Neutral Flame

The neutral flame occurs when the balance between oxygen and acetylene is equal. All the acetylene is being burned and the maximum heat is being produced. Almost all your welding will be with a neutral flame. Remember that the temperature in the hottest part of the flame (at the end of the inner cone) reaches 3,200 degrees C. The temperature at the outside end of the outer cone can reach just over 2,000 degrees C. Mild steel, the sort you will be welding, melts at about 1460 degrees C.

Oxidising Flame

The oxidising flame occurs when there is more oxygen than acetylene in the mixture. The inner cone becomes smaller and the torch produces a loud hiss as the oxygen level increases. This type of flame is used to cut steel and can be recognised by lots of sparks. It is never used to weld, and the only time you will use an oxygen-rich mixture is when you turn the oxygen level up to cut through a piece of scrap steel, such as on a rusty chassis or frame. This is discussed in another Chapter.

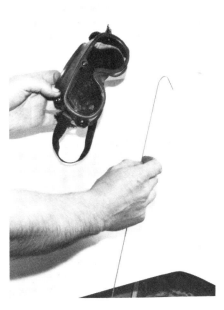

No welding text would be complete without the plastic bottles! You keep water in them, and they are handy for damping down hot steel. A good squeeze will direct a jet of water into a tight corner and help prevent a fire. For fire prevention information, contact your local FIRE PREVENTION OFFICER.

Two important safety items. The goggles protect your eyes; you CANNOT weld without them. The bent end of the welding rod reminds you that the other end is HOT, and stops you sticking the rod in your eye when you take the goggles off.

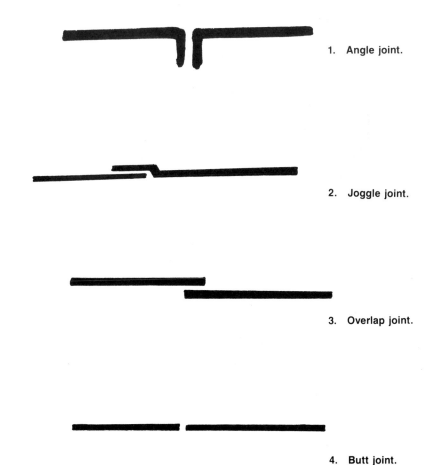

1. **Angle joint.**

2. **Joggle joint.**

3. **Overlap joint.**

4. **Butt joint.**

Appearance

One of the things I found most off-putting when I began serious metalwork was the appearance of the half-finished job. It would look burnt, rusty, dirty, untidy — in fact all the things were wrong that could be wrong. This can lead the amateur to a state of near dispair, wondering if he is doing things right and if they will ever look other than home repaired.

The secret is to do neat welding. Once you get into the habit of welding as neatly as possible, you will find that your finished jobs look better, and as we said right at the beginning, the neater the job the greater the satisfaction.

It helps if you have some sort of grinding tool to clean up the welds. However, this does not matter if you are welding a chassis or frame which will never be seen again. I'm thinking more of welding on external panels, or floor panels where your work may be noticed. Take a look at some of the 'half-finished' jobs in this book and you will see what I am talking about.

It is surprising though, how quickly a job heals up and blends in with the rest of the car. One day you have an ugly rusty hole in the floor, the next a neat patch welded in. You know where it is. You think everyone else will too. Paint the patch, then underseal it or put a sheet of bitumen over it. In six months time if I asked you to show me the patch you will only be able to show the approximate area — not the job itself.

In an earlier chapter we talked about 'shape'. In this section I will tell you a cheap and effective way of strengthening small patches by giving them some shape.

I use a shoemaker's last for this job, but that's only because I found an old one that nobody wanted. You can make up your own dolly to do the same job, or buy a 'shrinking dolly'. What you need is a flat piece of steel a couple of inches square with a shallow groove down the middle. I made my groove with a grinding stone in an electric drill. It takes a little while to get the right shape and depth, but a good guide is the 'ball' end of a hammer. This ball, or pein, to give it its proper name, should just fit into the groove you make.

The idea is that you lay a piece of metal over the groove. Hammer the steel so that the unsupported section (lying over the groove) is forced down into the groove.

The half-finished job... Looks terrible, doesn't it? In a few weeks you won't even remember where you welded — if you do neat work.

This Morris Minor emerges after six years in a garage. It is basically sound, but needs a little work on the door, and round the front panel.

Putting some shape into a small repair section. This home-made tool has served me well over the years. You can make one very easily, and produce...

This gives the panel extra shape and extra strength. It also gives a home-made panel a little extra style. Once again the photographs show you what to do. You can achieve a similar result by having a piece of steel with a hole in it. Hammer your panel down into the hole, moving it along until you develop a groove.

Hammer Welding

This technique is used a lot in the USA. Basically it consists of running a short length of weld then hammering the weld between a hammer and dolly. Some authorities on the subject say that this hammering strengthens the weld.

A good place to use this technique is when welding a repair panel along the bottom of a door. Its a long, almost flat area which would be subject to severe distortion problems with any other method. Hammer welding will not guarantee to get rid of distortion, but it will help.

I have used this technique for other reasons, long before I found out about it from

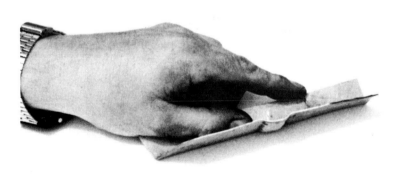

...shapes like this. The groove provides a lot of extra strength to the repair section. It also gives it a more professional finish.

Not rust damage, but a good workman could save this wing, rather than replace it. The first step would be to 'rough out' the damage with a heavy dolly. This would knock the panel back into approximately the right shape. (Photo Mark Hill)

a book. If you hammer a weld while it is still hot, you will flatten it quite easily, and this in itself gives you a neater finish. Don't strike the weld too hard, and don't strike it if it is not supported by a dolly. If you do it will buckle and you will have extra problems getting it right again.

Here's how to do it. First, you will need some tools. You need a hammer, (not your best panel-beating hammer — you may damage the face on stubborn welds) and a dolly. Also, you need a welding torch and ideally a rack or an assistant to hold the lit torch while you hammer. It is a three-handed job, so if you have to do it yourself, be prepared to shut off the torch between welds.

Clamp the two sheets to be joined as closely as possible. Tack weld them together in between the clamps. (A tack is a little spot of weld — just enough to fuse the two edges together to hold them in position). You want as small a tack as possible. Now run a bead of weld about an inch or two inches long. Switch off the torch (or give it to your helper) and place the dolly under the weld. Now strike the weld with the hammer, making sure that the dolly is underneath the hammered area. You should find that the weld will flatten quickly. Only a few blows with the hammer will be needed. Then pick up the torch, run another weld and so on. Repeat

the process until the job is done. You actually score in two ways with hammer welding. Because you hammer the weld, it is flatter and easier to finish with a grinder or a skim of glass fibre. The second reason is that because you only do short runs of weld, there is less heat build up and hence less distortion.

You may find a bucket of water helpful in case the dolly starts to get too hot to handle. You could always slow down if this happens! It would probably help if you wore a glove to hold the dolly. It's amazing how all sorts of hot debris you didn't know was there starts to fall on your hand when you hammer.

If you find that your early attempts are not too successful, try reducing the heat from the torch. There are two ways to do this. Either turn the heat down by adjusting the nobs, or lay the torch at a flatter angle to the steel. Instead of holding it at 60 degrees (approximately) try lying it almost parallel with the steel. You will find that it takes a long time to build up heat this way so, very gently, tilt the torch some more until the steel heats up.

Once you have finished a run with the torch and have hammered it down, stand back and have a good look. Is it a better job than you would have done without the hammer and dolly? Only you and your

experience can decided. Certainly I use the technique a lot, especially where it will be seen, such as on outer panels.

The weld should be easy to finish with a grinder. If you find that there are some low spots (areas lower than the surrounding surface, and not shiny after being sanded) try working them up with the hammer and dolly, this time putting the dolly on the 'high' side. (High spots are areas above the surrounding surface level). Gently work the hammer round the low side to bring it up to the level required. Don't worry if it is not perfect, you can always fill a small depression with filler. This would be quite acceptable if you gave the job to a professional, so don't worry about it.

Blobbing

I'm afraid I don't know the proper name for this technique. I was shown it by a professional panel-beater a number of years ago, and its one of those techniques that you keep on using again and again. Say, for example, you have welded a panel and have found that there are a few pin holes of rust you missed during your inspection. Before you reach for the glass fibre, consider this method.

Take a welding rod of either 1/16 inch or 1/8 inch, depending on the size of the hole.

Very gently heat the end of the rod, while keeping a little heat on the metal with the hole. When the end of the rod gets to the right temperature, it starts to expand. If you have ever seen someone blowing glass you will know what I mean. The end of the rod starts to bulge and go towards white heat. What you want to happen is for the blob of molten metal to fall from the welding rod onto the hole. The hole needs to be hot. Not too hot or you will burn a bigger hole. Just hot enough to accept the molten metal.

I have tried to explain this the best way I can, but the best thing to do is try it. Drill a few 1/16 inch holes in a bit of scrap steel and have a practice. Once you get it right, you will find that it will get you out of all sorts of tricky situations. I have never seen this technique explained anywhere, so have a practice at 'blobbing' next time you light the torch.

Cutting

Another very useful technique which is not often mentioned is how to cut small amounts of metal using the welding torch. Basically its a cheats method, but it has several advantages over a cutting torch.

For example, if you are welding in a piece of steel and you discover that you have cut the patch a little too large. You could either change the welding nozzle to a cutting nozzle and cut off the extra steel. In doing so you would create a lot of excess heat and run the risk of damaging the job. Try this instead. With the torch adjusted for welding, gently turn up the oxygen level. The torch will start to hiss and the flame will get smaller and fiercer. Direct the point of the flame to the steel to be cut. It will heat up (just as though you were welding) but will start to oxidise due to the excess oxygen. Move the torch in the direction of the cut. You will find that the welding torch will make a nice neat cut on the sort of thicknesses of steel we are talking about. Don't overdo things or you will again run into distortion problems.

Once again the best way is to try it on a piece of scrap.

Plug Welding

Plug welding is an interesting little technique which can get you out of trouble on many occasions. You need two pieces of steel, one of which has a hole drilled through it. The idea is you weld through the hole to the underlying sheet and in doing so join the two sheets.

It's best if you try it on a couple of bits of scrap. Take a bit of scrap steel a few inches on each side and drill a 1/8 inch hole anywhere in the steel. Next, clamp the two pieces of steel together, allowing yourself room to get the welding torch near the hole.

The front panel on this Capri has been built up from a number of small sections...

...while this close-up shows where Plug Welding has been used to fasten two sections. This job took a couple of hours and saved the front panel.

Heat the lower sheet of steel through the hole. You can tell when it is getting red hot by its appearance. When this happens, melt in some filler rod so that the filler rod melts into the lower sheet, and the upper sheet, leaving a nice neat weld. Once you have tried a sample on scrap steel, try to break it (once it cools, of course!). You might find your first attempts come apart, due to not achieving enough penetration on the lower sheet. Try again. Practice makes perfect, and scrap steel is quite cheap.

'Leapfrog'

There is no obvious place to define this

method of working, and you will see it mentioned throughout the book. Leapfrogging is the name I give to welding a small part of a job, leaving it to cool and moving the torch to another part of the job. In this way heat does not build up in one area and cause distortion. Weld a bit, leave a space, weld a bit, leave a space, and so on. After a time you will be 'leapfrogging' over a weld to weld in the area in front or behind it. Eventually, the job will be seam-welded, and hopefully not distorted!

Brazing

Why braze when you can weld, I always ask. However, there may be occasions when you feel you want to braze something rather than weld it. I am told that brazing is the correct technique when joining tubes in a tubular chassis. The only time I brazed any tubes was to mend a chair with a tubular frame!

Never kid yourself that brazing is a substitute for welding. It isn't. In brazing the two pieces of metal being joined are not fused together. To put things crudely, they are actually 'stuck' together using a bronze filler rod as the 'glue'. As with welding you **MUST WEAR GOGGLES** when brazing.

The advantages of brazing are that a much lower temperature is used, so distortion can be greatly reduced. Also material with a high carbon content can be brazed.

Material to be brazed must, ideally, be overlapped and be clamped tightly together. It is possible to braze a butt-joint, but it is something I have never done and wouldn't like to recommend to you.

Anyway, the secret of brazing is clean surfaces. The two pieces to be joined must be ultra-clean. A good rub over with a file or other abrasive is ideal. When the surfaces are clean, heat them both to a dull red using the welding torch.

Have the brazing rod handy (most rods have a flux coating which helps the molten rod to flow) and make sure that the torch is adjusted to give a neutral flame. Don't be tempted to use lots of brazing rod. A little will do the job just as well, if not better. The brazing rod will melt and if the temperatures are correct, should flow by capillary action between the two surfaces. The brazing material will actually fuse into the surface of the steel and provide quite a strong join.

If you want to try brazing the best way is to get hold of some bits of scrap steel and have a practice. You will learn more in half an hour with the torch in your hand than you will reading any book!

Cornered?

Sometimes, if you are welding into a corner or restricted space, you will find the

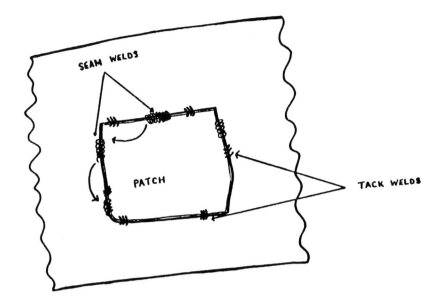

How to "leapfrog" when welding-in a patch.

flame keeps blowing out. This is because the burning gas is being directed into a tight corner, and cannot escape. Pressure builds up and snuffs out the flame. The answer is really simple, once you know it! Drill a tiny hole in the corner, to allow the gas pressure to 'leak' away. You won't have any more trouble. Don't worry if you can't fill it in later. A couple of heavy coats of paint will seal the size of hole I'm talking about.

Panel Beating

Panel beating is one of those mysterious areas that do-it-yourself types are reluctant to get involved in and it can make the average restorer reach for the plastic filler.

Professional tradesmen are not taught the old skills, as new vehicle design encourages replacement rather than repair. However there is still a lot the amateur restorer can do to a damaged panel. If a spare wing from the breakers yard is available then a few hours practice will improve your technique no end.

Assessing the Damage

Since this book only deals with rust damage and minor parking damage, you will have to decide if major work has to be handed over to a professional – and if it is worth the cost. Major accident damage calls for expensive jigs and highly skilled technicians to put right. One job which you can tackle at home is bumping out dents.

A dented front wing is probably the most common panel beating job which you can tackle. If the wing is not too badly damaged it can be repaired, but it pays to check out the rust damage before you

The Wheeling machine can produce all sorts of repair panels when operated by a skilled man. These machines are now hard to find.

start. Doors too, can take a lot of damage over the years and can often end up with lots of minor scars. Small dents in doors can be tackled at home, but access to the back of the panel is often difficult due to trim, winding mechanisms and glass.

Rear wings present more of a problem, as they are often double-skinned – that is a second sheet of metal lies immediately behind the outer panel. This makes it much more difficult to repair and generally the best that can be done is to fill the dent with plastic filler if it is not too deep.

Front and rear skirts or valances often suffer parking damage but this usually quite straightforward to repair. Bonnets and boots are normally double-skinned so a replacement from a breakers yard may be the cheapest alternative. Repairs can be done, but two layers of metal can be difficult to coax back into their correct positions.

Remember that any work done on an external body panel will show up right away if it is not done properly, and this will undoubtedly reduce the value of the car.

Outlining Damage

Let's run through the main steps in repairing a dented front wing. The first job is to define the area of damage. Sometimes this is not so easy to do, but if you are in any doubt, try this tip. Spray the area you think is damaged with an aerosol primer (any colour will do, as you will be rubbing it off later). You will find it dries pretty quickly, so after a few minutes wrap a piece of abrasive paper around a dowl, or piece of round brush-handle. Alternatively, if you have a large flat file, or better still a body file, use that to rub over the painted area. What will happen is that the 'normal' level of the panel will have the primer rubbed off, while the dent or low spot will remain painted. In this way you can determine where the low areas are.

Having defined the damaged area, and checked the rest of the panel for rust damage, you are now almost ready to tackle the dent.

Removing Underseal

If you started to work on the wing now, you would find lumps of dirt, debris, underseal, gravel — in fact all sorts of nasties. You have to remove them from the area to be worked on. Do this with scrapers and wire brushes. Some petrol on a rag will soften most types of underseal and make removal easier.

If you are working near a headlamp, remove it otherwise the vibration of hammering may damage the bulb or filament.

So now you have a nice clean area under the dent, and a marked out area on the outside of the panel. You can now try to 'rough out' the damage.

Roughing Out

Roughing out is the technique where you try to thump out the damage with a few *well-chosen blows* with a heavy dolly. If this is successful it may save you a lot of time with the hammer and dolly. The rule is to try to *reverse* the cause of the damage exactly. The deepest part of the dent was caused by the greatest force so this is the point to try to reverse the damage.

If you don't have the time or the skills, major restoration work can be done by professionals.

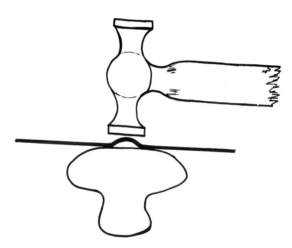

In Direct Hammering, the dolly is placed on the other side of the dent being worked. The steel is hammered against the dolly, whilst...

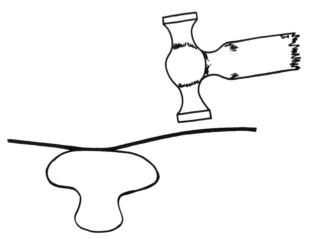

...in Indirect Hammering the hammering is done adjacent to the dolly, not against it. Both these methods are combined to work unwanted dents out of body panels.

Support the front of the panel with the palm of your hand and strike the damaged area at its deepest point. This is where the professional scores, as years of experience will direct his hand right to the correct spot, while you might be an inch or two out! An old scrap wing is ideal to practice on.

When you have roughed out the damage as best you can its time to use the hammer and dolly, unless you have been very lucky or very skilled and removed the dent. You are now ready to try metal bumping.

Bumping

Metal bumping is a general name given to metal shaping or panel beating. With the type of job described above, like on a front wing, I would normally place the dolly on the outside surface of the panel, and hammer the underside. If I hammer the area directly under the dolly the technique is know as 'direct hammering' or 'hammering on'.

If I hammer an area near to the area supported by the dolly, the technique is called 'indirect hammering' or 'hammering off'. Both techniques are used depending on the dent, where it is located, ease of access and so on.

Direct Hammering

This is probably the most widely used technique. You place a steel dolly over the dent and from the other side of the panel hammer the low part of the steel. The hammer blows must strike the steel squarely otherwise more damage will be done. Gently tap the low part of the dent in towards the dolly. With a bit of practice you should be able to coax the dent almost smooth again. If the dent is deep or severe the steel may have stretched and you will have to try another technique known as shrinking to try to cure it. More about shrinking later.

Indirect Hammering

This technique is used with certain types of dent. It consists of placing the dolly on the dent and hammering the adjacent area. The dolly should rebound from the hammer blow and strike the steel from underneath. The hammer blow is really only causing the dolly to rebound. In this way the dolly moves the steel back to the required level.

Both techniques need a lot of practice, and at the risk of repeating myself, you should spend some time with a scrap wing or panel to get the hang of things before starting work on your car.

Shrinking

This technique actually has two names, with both being widely different. Hot shrinking is the process where a stretched

The Grid Dolly is used to shrink stretched steel. It is part of the Hot Shrinking technique. (Courtesy Sykes-Pickavant)

The Shrinking Dolly is used during the Cold Shrinking process. This technique is easier for the amateur to master. (Courtesy Sykes-Pickavant)

sheet of metal is brought back into shape by the careful application of heat followed by a special hammering technique.

Cold shrinking consists of using a dolly with a groove in it, and hammering the stretched steel into the groove. This is then filled with lead or plastic filler. Let's look at hot shrinking in more detail first.

Hot Shrinking

Let's assume that you are going to practice on an old wing. The first job is to clean off any underseal or paint from underneath the damaged area. When this is done, get the tools ready, for they need to be handy

for some quick changes between one and another.

Using the welding torch with a number 1 or number 2 tip, heat a small area of the stretched panel. An area of about an inch in diameter is enough to start with. Bring this area to a bright red heat, by holding the torch tip vertically above it.

Now quickly put the torch down on a rack, or shut it off. Place a dolly under the hot spot and strike the steel around the spot with a mallet or hammer. This will force the stretched steel into the hot spot. The final mallet blows should be on the hot spot itself.

Repeat this procedure perhaps half a dozen times round the stretched area, cooling the area with wet rags between shrinks. The stretch should reduce and the panel regain its correct shape. Once again, it is a skill which takes time to master, so don't worry if your first attempts are not successful. It is better to make a mistake on a scrap panel, than on your car.

Cold Shrinking

This technique is much easier for the amateur to master, as it only needs a hammer and dolly. The dolly needs to have a groove down one face, and you can buy special shrinking dollies already made. However, you can make one from a piece of steel, an electric drill and a grinding stone. Just grind a groove in the face of the steel, about 1/4 inch deep. The groove needs smooth sides and no sharp edges. You now have a shrinking dolly!

Place the dolly on the underside of the damaged panel. Using a small hammer, tap the steel panel so that it is pushed down into the groove in the dolly. As the steel moves to fill the valley, the surface of the panel will flatten out and regain most of its shape. Be careful not to overdo things. Once you have the surface in reasonable shape, you will find that the rear of the panel now has a ridge or rib which will strengthen the panel.

When you are satisfied with the finish of the panel, prepare the outside of the panel and fill the groove with plastic filler, or lead if you have practised the technique. Remember to remove paint and roughen the surface being filled. It is possible, with careful rubbing down, to have an 'invisible mend' on a panel. Once again, have a go on a scrap panel before rushing out to your pride and joy!

Dent Pullers

A dent puller is simply a slide hammer. A self-tapping screw is screwed into a hole drilled in the low part of the dent. The self-tapper is fastened to the end of the dent puller. Hold the handle at the other end of the puller to steady the tool, then, keeping your fingers clear of the steel weight, sharply move the steel weight towards the handle end of the tool. This impact is transmitted to the self-tapping screw which pulls the dent out a little bit. Repeat the process until the dent starts to flatten out. I often find that the self-tapper pulls out of the steel before the job is finished, but this may work to your advantage if you have to use the technique a few times over the dent area.

Sometimes it is better to make a little hook to fit in the end of the puller. This can then be put into the hole and turned so that a more positive location is achieved.

This method works very well for lots of

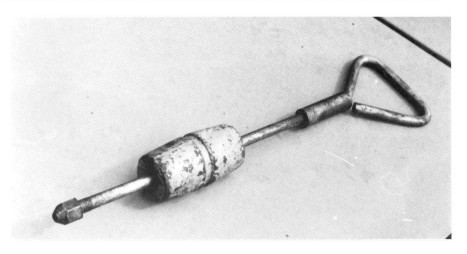

The dent puller, or slide hammer can be used to work out small dents. A self-tapping screw is fitted to the business end of the puller and screwed into the dent.

I'm making my own dolly from this lump of steel. I'll put a shallow groove across the top face, to give me my own, 'custom' dolly!

people, but I must admit its not my favourite.

Finishing Off

When you are satisfied that you cannot work the dent out any more – stop. It is pointless to keep on hammering as all you will do is stretch the panel which means more work. It is better to leave a shallow dent which is ideal for filling with plastic filler.

If you have a file or body file, work it over the repaired area to see if there are any high spots. A high spot is an area which has risen above the level of the panel. Use the file in an X pattern. First file in one direction, then at right angles to it. This will give a clearer picture of how the metal is lying. If there are any high spots they will show up shiny, as the file rubs over

them. These high spots will have to be gently tapped down again to achieve a better contour. Better to be low than high!

It may be worth trying a 'slapper' at this time. A slapper is simply a flat tyre lever which can be bought as a special panel-beating tool under the name of spoon. The slapper spreads the blows over a larger area causing less damage to the panel. Slap down any high spots revealed by the file. Remember to support the panel underneath with a dolly.

When you are satisfied you have done the best you can with the dent, clean up the surrounding area with a sanding disc in an electric drill. Remove paint from the surrounding area and clean off any surface rust which may have formed. For details of what to do to finish off the job see the Chapter, 'Paint and Protect.'

Rocker Panels/Sills _____

A nice shiny new sill ready to be welded into place. Mr Spate must have been the man who ordered the sills, but never got them! I got them cheap at an autojumble. Must finish that patch on the door...

The sills, or rocker panels as they are known in the USA, are normally a major part of a car's structure and must be treated as such. Unfortunately this does not happen and most 'restorable' cars feature great lumps of plastic filler in the sills. Sometimes things are so bad that the area between inner and outer sill is packed out with rags or newspapers then finished off with filler. *This is no good.*

In this Chapter I want to spend some time looking at sills, both outer and inner, inner wings and the A and B posts. (If you don't recognise these terms, they will be explained later in the Chapter). They don't fall into any other section of the book, so I will consider them to be part of the inner structure which can include sills.

One car I bought had sills which looked really good, but when I got down really close to look at them they looked a bit odd. I couldn't quite figure out what was wrong with them. Later when I got round to replacing them I found out what the problem was. There was a new 'outer' or sill

'skin' brazed over the original rusty sill. It looked almost right but bulges in the wrong place gave it away.

There is no short cut to restoring sills. Quite simply, they must be replaced. I don't consider it worth the time and effort to patch a sill. The only time I would consider doing this is if money was very tight, and I knew that the patch would complete the job satisfactorily. In any other case, replace the sill. Occasionally it is possible to repair local rust damage, but for the amount of extra trouble it is as well to replace the complete sill. That way, you can also have a look inside to see how the inner sill is standing up to the rust bug.

Lets say that we are going to replace a sill on one of my project cars. We will use this as an example and work our way through the job step by step. If I go wrong anywhere, you then have the knowledge to avoid my mistake and do a better job.

First thing to do is obtain a sill, or pair of sills for your car. Remember that the sills for a two door model may be different

from those used on the four-door version, so it pays to have a close look at any body catalogues you have. (This is where the manufacturer's Parts List comes in handy!).

It may be possible to use four-door sills on the two-door car with a bit of modification, but this is the sort of thing you have to be confident about before starting, OR get the relevant information from the Owners Club before you start.

Okay, you have two nice shiny sills in your hand and are ready to start. How long is it going to take? Well, whatever your estimate is, I would treble it, at least. If you think a couple of hours, forget it. It takes time to do work properly, but hopefully you will reap the rewards of another 20 years of happy motoring after the work is done.

Decide if you have to take the doors off. This will allow you better access to the sills but makes for extra work. On my two-door cars I tend to leave the door on and tie it open with a rope. This amuses the neighbours but allows me the best of both worlds; easy access, plus instant fitting of the door to see if it clears the new sills.

Offer up the new sill to the car and be sure that it is the correct sill. If in any doubt, make sure by contacting the supplier again. I'll make a bold statement here and say 'You can't drive the car once the old sill is chiselled off!' One other point. Don't try to do both sills at the same time. Work on one side until the job is completed – then start on the other side. If you cut both away at the same time you run the risk of seriously weakening the bodyshell.

Mark where the sill should fit the car, For example if you have a pattern sill rather than one made by the vehicle manufacturer, you may find that it does not have all the folds and steps of the original. This means you have to use part of the old sill to join the new sill. This is okay, but make sure you fully understand how you intend to fit the sill before you start.

Pay particular attention to where the sill meets the B post. (The A post is the vertical assembly which runs from the sill up the side of the windscreen on a conventional car. Normally it carries the hinges for the front door. The B post is in the middle of the side of the car, and on a four-door car carries the hinges for the rear doors. The C post is at the rear of the sill and carries the door shut mechanism for the rear doors.)

The A and C posts are generally at the ends of the sills and the sill maker will have made the sill to fit (we hope), but the middle (or B post) may well need individual attention. Be sure you know what to do here before you start. Later in the Chapter there is some more information about A and B post repairs.

Jack up the car and put it on axle stands or ramps, to give you a better view of the job. Do NOT use bricks to hold up a car. Make sure the stands are safe. Local newspapers are full of stories about people crushed by falling cars supported by bricks. Don't be one of them. There are better ways to get in the papers. A story about how you restored an old 'Ark-mobile' would be much more interesting than a story about being crushed under a car.

Before you lift a tool and start work, please run through the following checklist, which is designed to prevent trouble at a later stage of the job.

1) Have you removed all carpets, trim, underfelt, underseal and even paint which could catch fire when you start to weld?

2) Have you examined the area where the inner sill meets the floor, in case there is a run of wiring loom or harness? It is pointless burning through a wiring harness for the sake of a 30 second inspection.

At the front of the new sill, and a lot of work still to do on the inner wing. The new front chassis outrigger is in place and that inner sill repair plate will be cut to size later.

3) Are you confident you have thought your way through the job? Have you read all of this Chapter prior to tackling the job?

4) Have you got the correct sills for the year, make, model, etc of your car? If not, do you know how to make your sills fit?

5) Have you allowed plenty of time to do the job properly? I would allow one weekend per sill. If this sounds too much, remember I have been caught out plenty of times by saying the car would be back on the road in a couple of hours, only to find it jacked up weeks later waiting on something I had overlooked.

6) Do you have to make any alterations to the sill to allow access to jacking points?

7) Have you considered the possibility that what you think is the sill is just a decorative cover-plate, hiding the real sill underneath. Morris Minor owners take note!

8) If you cannot locate sills for your old car, have you remembered that a skilled metalworker with a metal bending machine can make them for you? All he needs is a pattern, such as cutting a 'slice' vertically through the old sill. From this he can decide the gauge of steel, and the shape. All you then need to tell him is how long it needs to be and when you want it.

9) Have you got all the welding gas, welding rods etc you will need to complete the job, especially if you are working on the car over the weekend when all the

suppliers are shut? (I don't want to put you off doing the job, but think it through first to avoid any grief later).

Once these problems are sorted out, get out the faithful hammer and chisel and start to remove the sill. If you have to use part of the top section of the original sill, mark a cutting line on the old sill and cut to that line with hammer and chisel or tin snips. There are several ways to remove a sill, here are some of mine:

If the sill is spot-welded along the top, where it meets the top of the inner sill, you can chisel through these spot welds quite readily to detach the sill.

If the sill is spot-welded along the bottom edge where it joins the bottom of the inner sill, you can   chisel these off quite readily.

If you have a power drill you can buy a spot weld removing tool for about £7. This drills into the spot weld and breaks it open. It needs a slow-turning drill, otherwise you will quickly blunt the tool. I have never used this method, but you may find it suits you.

Cut the sill off with a cutting torch. There are several reasons why you should not do this, but on occasion I have removed part of a sill with a cutting flame. The biggest

A typical nasty mess at the rear end of the sill. The inner sill has rotted away (you can see right through it) and those wisps of material suggest a previous glass fibre repair.

problem is distortion. You do not want to distort any part of the body you will be attaching the sills to.

As you start to get the old sill off, you will probably find it easier to cut the sill into pieces, so that you remove a section about a foot long at a time. This allows more controlled removal and you can then see the next problem before you get to it. For example, if you started to remove the outer sill as described above, then found that

there was no inner sill left due to rust, you would be in a safer position than if you just removed the entire sill in one piece. In other words, the car would not be weakened by the loss of the outer sill.

I would allow a couple of hours to get each sill off. Professionals may well laugh at this sort of time, but you are not in any hurry, are you?

Do it once, and do it right.

Don't throw the old sills away until the new ones are fitted. It is surprising the amount of information that this old sill will provide if you get stuck. Note the drain tubes through this sill.

This old sill has been chiselled off and you can see where each spot weld was cut along the bottom edge. Keep this sill handy until you drill the holes for the trim decoration in the new sill.

A view of an inner sill, with the outer sill which has been chiselled off, lying on the floor. This inner sill is in good condition and only needs the mounting flanges ground smooth before fitting new outers.

Two new sills ready to be fitted. These sills need to be welded to part of the old sill, but provide a neat finish.

Grind off the remains of any spot welds exposed, so that you have a nice, flush fit with the new sill when you come to fit it. Wear goggles when grinding. Beware angle grinders as they cause a lot of sparks which can embed themselves in windscreen glass and spectacles. Once in, you can never get them out. The glass feels rough to the touch. You have been warned.

When the sill is off, examine the inner sill. You may be unlucky and find that it requires major surgery or that it needs replacing. You should have discovered this from underneath the car, by looking at the exposed part of the inner sill. However even the most thorough inspection can sometimes miss corrosion, so don't worry too much. Having got this far the damage can be made good but it will just add extra time to the job.

Let's say that having got the outer sill off you need to repair the inner sill. A couple of patches will do the job. (You could replace the inner sill if one was available but this may not be necessary).

Scrape off all the rust from the inner sill. A wire brush in the electric drill is ideal for this. Once you have cleaned up the area, you can make another inspection to find out the extent of the damage. Mark the areas to be removed with a pencil or marker pen. Is the steel flat, or does it have shape? If it has shape, can you re-make that shape in your new repair section? Could you buy one inner sill and use half of it on each side of the car? Questions like this can save you a lot of money if you get the right answers.

Cut out one of the sections to be replaced. Keep it handy — do NOT throw it away. Lay it on top of a piece of fresh steel or make a paper template as described in Chapter One. Either way, make a repair patch which can be butt-welded into place. If the patch has shape, use your grooved dolly or some substitute to make a groove. (Remember to make the groove or ridge face the correct way!)

When the patch is ready, hold it in position with Mole welding clamps or whatever other suitable clamps you have available. Leave a 1/16 inch gap between the old and new steel to allow for distortion when welding.

Weld the patch into place. The welding will be easier if you have the car up on axle stands or ramps.

When the patch is welded in place, smooth off the welds as best you can, bearing in mind that access to the inner sill might not be very good. There is a temptation to say, 'No-one will ever see it, so why bother.' Work on the basis that someone WILL see it, and you will achieve better standards of work.

Follow the same technique for other patches. If you have to insert more than a couple of patches, think seriously about replacing the entire inner sill. It may be better in the long run. However, if money is tight, or the parts not available, then it will be all right to patch, provided you do a professional job.

You may find a heavy bracket, washer, or nut, spot welded to the inner sill. This is the seat belt mounting hole. This is a great opportunity to check the seat belt bolt and ensure that it can be removed from its captive nut. I would advise you to take the bolt out, give it a little brush with a wire brush to remove any dirt, oil it then refit it. It should be good for another 25 years. NOW is the time to discover a problem, not when the new sill is welded in place. I took the opportunity on my car to add a couple of heavy spot welds to the seat belt mounting plate, just to re-inforce it. You can see them in the photograph. When all is well with the inner sill, paint it with a couple of coats of rust-inhibitor or whatever your favourite protective paint happens to be.

Now, lots of people will argue that the paint will be burnt off when you weld on the new sill. I agree that some will, but it is a lot less than you think, especially if you use a heat resistant paint. Any paint is better than no paint, and you don't want to have to repeat the job in a few years time, do you?

Inner sill completed, it's time for a coffee, while you contemplate the fitting of the new outer sill. You should have smoothed off any exposed spot-welds left over from the removal operation. If not do so now, as a lumpy spot weld can upset the nice smooth lines of your new sill.

You are going to need a minimum of about four clamps to hold a sill in position, so get those organised now.

Offering Up

Offer the sill up to the car, and once it is roughly in position, clamp it in place with a couple of clamps. One on the bottom and one at the rear end will do to start with. Now check that the door will still clear the sill. I was caught out once before, when I fitted a Volvo sill. It was okay when I checked it, but when welding was complete the front corner of the door fouled the edge of the sill. Modifications were required and the language was choice! Don't get caught.

If everything is okay, and all the edges of the sill meet all the edges of the inner sill etc. you have been quite lucky. Often a sill will need slight modifications to make it fit properly. Normally these can be done

Make sure that the mountings for your seat belts are in good condition. This plate carries the lower mounting bolt on the Cortina. While the sill is off, check that the bolt can still be removed and has not rusted.

without too much worry, but the more you check early on, the less chance of hitting unexpected snags.

Now clamp the sill in position with as many clamps as are available to you. I have used as many as six before now, to ensure a good fit. Check again to make sure the door will still clear the sill and that the door line is even with the sill. To do this you might have to remove some of your clamps, depending on where you put them. There is no easy answer to this. You must check, and you must clamp. Just make sure that when you remove a clamp the sill does not move.

When you are entirely satisfied that the sill is correctly fitted, fit a number 1 nozzle to the torch, light up, and make a few tack welds. Half a dozen tack welds will allow you to remove the clamps and make a further check on sill location. If all is well, proceed to weld the sill into place. I normally seam-weld the entire length of the sill, but you may choose not to. If you have a spot-welder available (perhaps you can hire one for a day just to do the sills) make welds every half inch to an inch all along top and bottom of the sill.

Remember to leave drain slots on the bottom edge of the sill. Make them by leaving about half an inch un-welded, then put a screwdriver blade between the inner and outer sill. Give this a few twists and it will open up a neat drain slot. You don't want the sills to fill with water, do you?

Check the A, B and C posts of the car and weld these posts to the sill. If new patches have to be made up, make cardboard templates first. When the patch is tacked in place, make sure the door swings without fouling the patch. Make sure these patches are made neatly, as they will be seen. The A and B posts are covered in more detail later in the Chapter.

Your sills should have some sort of front and end piece, but if not you will have to fabricate the ends. Hopefully you still have the ends from the old sill to use as a pattern, but if not you will have to use intui-

A new sill welded onto this Capri, and the next job is to repair the damaged rear quarter panel. A new repair panel for this is available from the Consul Capri Owner's Club.

tion, guesswork, or sheer genius to make the ends. You could always look at another car of the same make and model. It's not the first time I have had to refer to my other Cortina when repairing the first one!

At the rear end of the sill the blanking piece or end piece normally blends into the sweep of the wheel arch, and onto the inner part of the wheel arch. If this sounds confusing, see the photographs. Your task is to make up a piece of steel to complete the job. If I were you, I would reach for the template materials as described in the first Chapter. It also helps a lot to scrape off any underseal or paint which would stop you welding properly.

Make absolutely sure that you have made the template as best you can. If you have to, make it over and over again until you are satisfied. Then cut steel. Don't use steel that is too thick. Try 18 gauge. While you are planning the end piece, consider if you can drill a large hole in the middle to allow access for a spray gun or tube. This will make protection of both inner and outer sill easier.

When the end piece is cut from steel, figure out a way to clamp it in position. I can't offer any specific advice on this as each car will vary in its design. I usually find I can get a hold with a pair of Mole Grips. This is enough to hold things in place while I get a couple of tack welds on.

WARNING: Before you start welding, check that there is no upholstery, underfelt or any other material within range of the welding torch.

Remember that heat travels a long way in a piece of steel such as a sill, so don't confine your checks too closely to the end of the sill. Remember that if a seat or trim panel catches fire it will spread so quickly that

A repair patch welded into the inner sill, adjacent to the outrigger shown in the photo below. Different car — same problem!

there is little you can do about it. This type of fire gives off choking fumes and before you realise it, you have a very nasty situation on your hands. Once again, a few sensible precautions will go a long way to prevent accidents.

Once you have a few tack welds holding the sill, begin to seam weld the panel in place. Do only short runs then shut off the torch and tap the weld and the end piece into place again, as the distortion caused by the heat will make the end piece buckle slightly. It is important to seam weld this end piece — and it is important to do it well. The reason is simple once it is pointed out to you. This area gets all the water, all the muck, all the debris from the road, thrown up by the wheel. You MUST do a sound job here, otherwise rust will start the next time you drive the car in the wet.

Once the sill is seam welded in position, get a couple of heavy coats of your favourite protective paint onto it as soon as the steel cools off. Rust can begin very quickly, depending on the air temperature.

At the front of the sill, things may be a little more difficult, as the sill may end almost inside the front wing. This means access is difficult or impossible. I have had to remove the spot welds holding the rear of the wing to the A post and then pull the wing out about six inches to gain access to the front of the sill. The photograph shows this well.

I can't give you any specific advice on this area, it depends so much on the make and model of the car. One thing you MUST NOT DO, is throw away the old sill. Keep all of it until you have finished replacing it.

A new outrigger in place and the next job is to repair the corrosion on the inner sill. You can see where I have already cut away some rusty material from the bottom edge.

It is amazing how much information a rusty old bit of steel can provide if you get stuck. As I said in the first Chapter, shape gives steel strength and style. If the rust takes the strength away, then the style and shape may still be there. Use this to help you make a new front piece.

Before I leave the subject of sills, I want to emphasise again that you must not work on both sides of the car at the same time. To do so would be to invite trouble. The entire bodyshell could become distorted if you cut out too much old steel at a time. Concentrate on one area, complete the work, then go on to the next. If you are worried about distorting a bodyshell then seek advice from a professional. Alternatively, you can use strategic lengths of timber to support weakened areas. Don't get too adventurous. If in doubt – ask.

Sills provide a lot of the strength in a bodyshell. Being an outer panel they are seen, and a pair of rusty old sills can spoil an otherwise perfect car. Don't abuse sills and don't overlook them. Allow plenty of time to restore them.

Sill Decoration

On some sills there are bits of chrome trim, or other decoration. These can often be difficult to replace if you are trying to restore a car to 'as new' condition. On the old Ford Capri and Classic there is a length of chrome strip about two inches wide which is fastened to the sill by plastic fasteners. I'm not sure if you can still obtain these fasteners, so if you have removed an old sill make sure you recover any items like this before you throw it away. That's another good reason for not using heat to remove a sill. In this case you would have burnt the plastic fasteners and caused yourself extra work.

There is another good reason for keeping the old sill. You need it as a pattern to use when drilling new holes in the sill for the plastic fasteners.

A and B Posts

Just to refresh your memory the A post is the pillar or structure on which the front door hinges. (Unless you have an older car with forward opening doors).

The B post is the structure in the middle of a 4-door car which locates between the sill and the roof. On a 2-door car the B post is usually part of the rear quarter panel.

If you have rust problems at the bottom of the A or B posts, they can be repaired quite readily. If you have rust in the

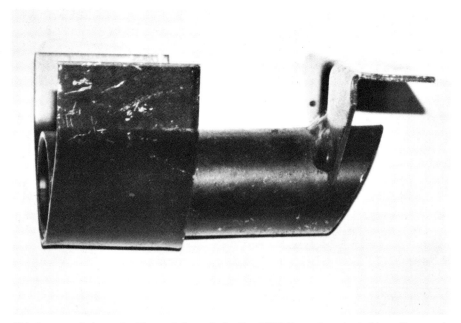

This is a good strong jacking point, made for the MGB. It can be adapted to suit several other cars. I have used one on the front outrigger of my Capri to produce a functional replica of the rusted out original.

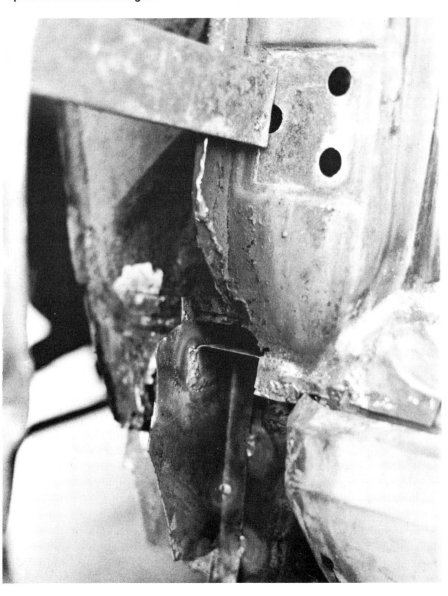

Some rebuilding work at the bottom of the inner wing, where it meets the inner sill. The piece of steel is keeping the wing clear of the work area.

middle of B post it can be repaired easily. However, things start to get a little tricky now. If you have rust in the middle of the A post, adjacent to the top of the inner wing and close to the windscreen aperture, you might have problems. The repair work can be done, but there will be a lot of extra mechanical work to be done, including removal of the windscreen.

If you have rust at the top of the A or B post, you again have problems. Not because the welding is difficult. No, its because of that nice headlining which is highly inflammable and will have to be removed first. This is a tricky job on many cars, and not one I would like to tackle very often. You may also find that some wiring is run up through the windscreen pillar and this might have to be removed before you can weld.

(A quick tip if you have to do this. Locate the end of the wire at the top of the pillar. It may go to an interior light. Get an old

Same area as the lower photo, opposite, but more work has been done. The inner wing has been repaired, as has the front of the inner sill. The wing can now be welded back in place.

On the other side of the car there are similar problems. The A Post has been repaired at the bottom, and is about to be fixed to the sill by another (curved) patch piece.

The rear end of the sill, where it meets the rear quarter panel. New patch pieces have been fabricated and welded in place. A little more work is needed to blend the repair into the flange on the top of the sill.

The B Post, and a small repair patch has been welded between the lower edge of the post and the sill. A further small patch is needed to the right, to complete the repair.

piece of wire, or even a thin welding rod. Tape the old wire or welding rod to the electrical wire. Be sure it is a secure join, and not too bulky, as it will have to pass down the screen pillar. Pull the electrical wire from the bottom, feeding the old wire or welding wire down from the top. When the join emerges from the bottom you know you can weld away without damaging the vital wire. When the job is done, reverse the procedure and re-connect the wire to the light fitting).

Lets first assume that you have been lucky and that your A and B posts have suffered some tin-worm near the bottom, where they meet the sill. Your biggest weapon here is the humble template. Get some card templates made up of the repair sections needed BEFORE you cut out any steel. Make sure they are accurate too.

If you find that you have some awkward shape to make, with double curves, consider making it in two pieces and welding it together. This may look more difficult to do, but it will save you sitting there until next Christmas with a pile of scrap metal beside you trying to make a shape which is beyond your capablilites!

Having made templates accurately, cut them out from steel. When they measure up nicely against the originals, cut out ONE piece from the post. By one piece, I mean one side of the post. Clean up your cut and attend to any rust damage on the inner sill hidden by the post. Locate the first patch and tack it into place.

Check again that it is correctly located, then having allowed it to cool, try opening and closing the door. Make sure you have not caused any problems about fit. The reason for waiting till the welds cooled was to prevent you melting the door seal rubber! Yes, guess who found out the hard way! Also check that any sill decoration or kick plate which might be attached to the sill top will still fit with the patch in place.

If in doubt, fit the kick plate and try closing the door. It's worth remembering here that your door hinges may well be worn, so lift the edge of the door to feel for movement in the hinges. You might need to make allowances for this before you carry on. If you have new door hinges available, fit them now and get the door fit correct before going on with the welding.

Weld the patch into position as neatly as you can. Remember it will be seen every time you open the door. If you do it neatly, you will forget about it after a couple of coats of paint.

Build up the complete repair job a bit at a time until it is complete. Then move to the next post and follow the same procedures.

You may find, as I did that this takes a bit longer than you expected. You will also find, as I did that the end result was well worth the extra effort.

That's the bottoms repaired. Nothing too difficult there, honestly! Now let's look at some rust in the middle of the A post, as shown in the photographs. There are a number of things to look out for here, such as electrical wiring and the possibility of starting a fire if there is any underseal or filler around the area.

If possible, remove the door. It will make life a lot easier for you. Decide the extent of the rust and cut out a template to size. Remember that all the rust must be removed, so make your inspection thorough and the template big enough. When you have the template ready, cut out the rust.

Unless you are very unlucky, you will probably find the rust quite localised. You might also find that an electric drill with a tapered grinding stone will aid cleaning up the rusted area.

When the rust is all cut out, check that the template still covers the rusted area. If that is still okay, cut out the steel patch. You can make it 1/16 inch smaller all round and weld it in flush with the surrounding steel, or put a simple patch overlapping existing steel. The choice is yours.

The bottom of the A Post and some serious rust. Much of this is due to leaks around the windscreen rubber, and water running down the inside of the A Post, and gathering at the bottom. Quite simple to repair though.

Although there are no sills to be seen on this unknown vehicle, I could not resist using the photo to remind you about 'shape' once again. Notice the way the mudguards are formed from various sections. Neat!

INNER WINGS

Inner wings are best treated as patching jobs, unless yours is so badly damaged that you need to consider replacement. You may find this sort of panel hard to find and expensive, so before you start to panic, have a real close look at the situation.

I will assume you have removed the wing and are now looking at the inner wing. Generally, rust will have attacked near the top and the bottom. Just to be difficult it may also have created little rust spots or holes in the middle of the panel too.

Top and bottom can be patched, the middle should be cut out and a patch let in. All the techniques you need are described elsewhere in the book.

Have a look in any body parts catalogues

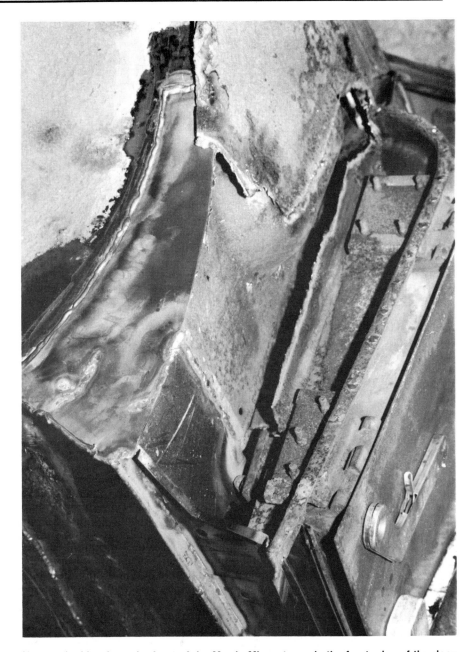

You are looking from the front of the Morris Minor, towards the front edge of the door post. The whole area is being restored on this car, with a new sill panel already welded in place at the bottom. (Photo by Roger Turner.)

A patch at the bottom of the windscreen pillar on a Cortina. Damage in this area is often caused by leaking windscreens.

Another view of the same area on the Morris Minor. Severe corrosion will mean a lot of work and many repair sections will be needed to revive this particular car.

This beautiful Lotus has an all-alloy body and a tubular steel frame. No rusty A Posts to fix on this car! Note the use of pop rivets to join body panel sections.

A rather sad 1937 Chevrolet Coach dying in a field in North America. Once the glass breaks, and the weather gets in, damage quickly gets worse. This example is probably past saving, but the chassis frame is still good and could be salvaged. (Photo by Mark and Terry Hill.)

you may have. Look to see if there are any repair panels for inner wings, and also think if one panel from another car may be adapted to save your inner wings. For instance, the Morris Minor has an inner front wing repair section which might well be adaptable on other similar cars.

On two of my cars I have had to put multiple-patches on the inner wings. If they had not been treated with special paint when they were new, they would never have survived twenty-odd years. Thanks to the original owners, the cars can be saved.

The money I paid for these cars has not justified searching for and paying for new inner wings. But it takes time and effort to cut and patch, and if you look at the job half-finished you can get put-off. Don't let that happen. If you get fed up, put the tools away and come back to it another day. In cases like this I pack up the welding tools and do something else, such as cut out some templates for another job. This keeps the overall restoration going, but allows you a rest from a particular area causing you headaches.

The main thing to look out for when working on inner wings is starting fires. Be absolutely sure that the inside of the inner wing is cleared of cardboard trim panels, lumps of bitumen sealer, electrical cables, cables to aerials, and any excess paint. Get rid of all of these before lighting the torch. If you don't the price you pay will be high. A fire under there will rise to the dashboard assembly and the main wiring loom. This could cost a lot of money to put right. Don't get caught out.

If you are in any doubt about finding any pin holes of rust, wait until it's dark and switch on an inspection lamp on the inside of the inner wing. Look for tell-tale points of light which will shine through holes or very thin bit of rusty steel.

Once you have completed the patching work, pay special attention to getting several thick coats of protective paint all over the area. The chances are, you will not be taking the wing off again in a hurry, so make sure all your efforts are protected. When paint has dried, underseal with a good heavy coat of bitument.

In the next Chapter we will look at chassis and frame repairs. It may not be an exciting subject, but there is a lot more you can do thanyou might at first think.

Export specification Cortinas had this additional bracket welded between the inner wing (at the strut top) and the bulkhead, for extra strength. Some cars used for rallying used a steel bar bolted between the strut tops for similar reasons. (Photo by Mike Pratt).

Ugh! Rust, rust, rust on this Morris Minor. Several panels form the sill assembly on the Minor, and it looks like every one of them has rusted on this example. Once again, it can be repaired by replacing a couple of sections. (Photo by Roger Turner).

Frame/Chassis Repairs

Looks terrible doesn't it? But with a bit of care and attention, plus some careful welding this chassis will live again for another 25 years. It has already been repaired, but the patch at the bottom must be removed and the job done properly.

This is one of the most interesting (I think!) and one of the most overlooked subjects in the whole world of vehicle restoration. I was never able to find a useful book on the subject, until Osprey Publishing got me to write 'How to Restore Chassis and Monocoque Bodywork' which, without being too big-headed, I think covers the subject pretty well.

For years I asked around garages and workshops to try to find someone who specialised in 'chassis welding' as it was known. Answers ranged from 'You must be joking mate, I tried it once and did my back in!' to 'Nobody round here does that sort of thing – better junk the car.'

I finally found a man, working in a little wooden lock-up garage who specialised in chassis repairs. He worked six days a week, had more than enough work to keep him busy and he is now driving around in a Rolls Royce. He helped me a lot at the beginning and proved to me that it can be a dirty, unpleasant, miserable task. However, there are ways to make things easier... So, over the years I have done a lot of chassis welding on various cars and anything I tell you in this Chapter is hard-

won personal experience. If I can do it, so can you, since I do not claim to have any special skills.

Being a problem area has its advantages. There are still a lot of people who think chassis welding is a black art which only a few eccentrics can do. This means you can buy the car cheaper and do the work yourself. One of the specialised books on my bookshelf shows a picture of a rusty chassis section and the caption advises the reader to avoid a car with this sort of damage. *Absolute rubbish!* The same book advocates spending hundreds of pounds welding on new wings and sills, so why can't you apply the same principles to the frame or chassis?

Later in this Chapter, I will guide you through a couple of typical chassis repairs which the do-it-yourself man can tackle with confidence. Also, the Ford Cortina photo-spread shows lots of chassis repairs and this was all done without any special equipment or skill. I don't believe I have any special skills that no-one else has. I have some experience, true, but there is nothing to stop you gaining experience of a particular aspect of restoration. If you

want a car of the 1950s or 1960s, then you are going to have to learn some chassis welding skills. The sooner you start, the sooner you have experience.

I like to think of a chassis as the skeleton of the car. If you think of a U-shaped piece of steel with half inch lips, described in the first Chapter as a Top Hat, you will have a very good idea of the general shape of a chassis member.

Various lengths, sizes and styles of the above section are combined in the factory to form a chassis. If you have appreciated the simplicity of the above, can you now mentally add a 'lid' to the box?

You have added the 'floor' and now have a chassis member attached to the floor. These basic building blocks make up the modern monocoque car. The result is very strong but very light. Typically the gauge (or thickness) of the steel would be 14, 16 or 18 gauge, (2mm, 1.6mm or 1.2mm) for chassis sections and 20 or 22 gauge (1mm or 0.8mm) for outer panels. Note, these are only approximations and will vary according to the type of car.

If we extend this idea just a little further and say that normally each length of chassis is perhaps one foot long increasing to three or four feet , it becomes a practical proposition to remove one rusty section at a time and weld in a new one. I'm not suggesting you rush out and remove three feet of your chassis. What I am saying loud and clear is that a car with chassis rust damage CAN be repaired by the do-it-yourself restorer.

This might be a suitable point to remind you that you can use second-hand chassis parts to repair your car. If you can find a clean, rust-free section on a car in the breaker's yard, there is no reason why you should not cut it out of the wreck, clean it up and weld it into your car. This can save a lot of money as well as being the only source for rare parts.

Assuming you have found the parts you need, or can adapt something else, let's have a look at what is involved in chassis repairs.

INSPECTING THE DAMAGE

Before you start removing sections of the chassis, remember that they are welded to floor sections. If a chassis member is rusty, there is a very good chance the floor section will be rusty too. When examining a chassis for rust, you must make absolutely sure you know the extent of the rust. Look at least six inches all round the suspect chassis section. Clean off underseal too, as it can often hide rust. In fact some second-hand dealers probably think its main purpose is to hide rust!

Scrape and prod the chassis member with a screwdriver. I have an old one especially for this purpose. If there is rust, be prepared to renew the section.

When you are sure you know which bits are solid steel, and which bits are rusty, get ready to remove the rusty bits. Remember that one piece of chassis probably attaches to a floor section, and possibly to two other pieces of chassis section as well. Make sure you know if your repair section has enough lips or flanges to join other sections, or if you will have to add little joining patches. This sort of detail can add hours to a job which at first looks simple.

REMOVING SECTIONS

To remove a rusty section you need a 2-lbs hammer and a 4-inch flat chisel and a pair of clear protective goggles. Sounds drastic? Yes, it is but why waste time on rusty metal?

Insert the chisel BETWEEN the lip on the chassis section and the floor section. You can usually force it into the spaces between spot-welds. Having gained access, hammer through the spot-welds to release the section. You can cut through the chassis

HOW TO RESTORE
Chassis and Monocoque Bodywork

Osprey Restoration Guide 9

Tommy Sandham

I wrote this book for Osprey Publishing in 1985 and I believe it is the only book which covers the subject of chassis and monocoque repairs. American readers will know that 'Unibody' means the same as 'monocoque'.

section next to the lip, and leave the lip welded to the floor. Sometimes you have to do this because of difficult access with the chisel. You MUST remove this remaining strip of metal before you weld in the new section. Try winding it round a pair of pliers, like opening a can of sardines. This usually breaks the spot welds.

The chassis section will also be welded onto the next section of chassis. If you have a new repair section available, mark where you need to cut after measuring the new section. If you are going to make a new repair section, then cut at a suitable point.

The chassis might fasten to the inner sill. Examine the join and decide how to fit the new section.

Sometimes a hacksaw will help the removal process, and sometimes I cheat a little and use the welding torch with an oxygen-rich flame to cut stubborn pieces of chassis. Take your time on this, and be warned: it will take longer than you think!

You are always left with a pile of rusty metal, dirt, dust and debris on the floor of the garage and you are left wondering where the chassis part went.

Having removed the old section, make a final inspection for rust, as all that hammering might have shown up some more weak spots. It is also useful to go over the area with a wire brush in the electric drill. This cleans up the area and highlights any bits needing attention, such as a spot weld needing to be ground down. A grinding stone in the electric drill often works better in this sort of situation, as it get into tighter corners than the angle grinder. Make sure you get it all smoothed off.

I'll assume now, that you have bought a replacement chassis section from a motor factors and that you are ready to fit it. I'll also assume that you are puzzled about how you hold the section in position prior to welding!

The simple answer is, jack it up! Put a simple screw jack under the chassis section

The Morris Minor front end, showing serious rust problems round the front of the main chassis member and on the tie plate. This looks bad, but can be repaired by fitting some new parts as shown in...

...this photo, which was taken as the new chassis member and tie plate is tack welded in position. This plate will be seam welded to the other parts of the chassis and will provide a sound repair which will last a long, long time. (Both photos by Roger Turner.)

Here a new outrigger is trial fitted in position. A new floor panel has been welded in place, and the old part of the floor has yet to be trimmed off. Two clamps and a screw jack hold everything firmly together.

and gently raise the jack until the chassis is in position. It might take a few attempts to get it right but it should fit eventually. If it does not fit, perhaps the floor panel is distorted due to your hammering.

Another way to locate a chassis member is to drill two holes in the floor, one on either side of the chassis member and close to the half inch lips. Place the chassis in position and put a nut and bolt through the hole.

When you tighten up the bolt, you should clamp the chassis against the floor. You might need to use a couple of washers to get the clamping action spread over a decent sized area. You can fill the holes in later with weld.

Once the chassis section is in position, make a final check for fire hazards before lighting the torch. Look out for wiring looms which can become camouflaged with years of dirt and cigarette ash! Don't spoil the job for a few minutes' inspection. Lie on the ground and make a few tack welds to hold the chassis to the floor. For this sort of work I would use a number 2 tip in my torch, or even a number 3 if I felt that the floor or chassis section were of heavier gauge steel. Once you have done this, remove the jack and make a final

check that the chassis section is exactly in its correct position relative to the floor, and to the inner sill or main chassis member. If not, put matters right now. Remove the tack welds if you have to, but get it right!

Once the section is located correctly, seam weld it into position. I like to run a few inches of weld, then move the torch to another part of the section and run an inch or so there. In this way I do not build up too much heat in any one area. Now and again, shut off the torch, tap the floor section down and tap the chassis section up to ensure that the lip on the chassis makes a nice flat contact with the floor. Once its all welded in place – and again this can take much longer than you expect due to physical discomfort – get some paint on it to prevent rust starting.

For this sort of work you need to get as comfortable as possible. I like to rest my head on something such as a spare tyre or a bundled up overall. Anything will help.

Chassis Repairs

Let me talk you through two actual chassis repair jobs which you should be able to tackle if you can run a reasonable weld.

The first job is a big one, and had been done badly before I bought the car. I believe 'cheap and cheerful' is the phrase, but to me it looked cheap and nasty. It was the sort of welding I have come to expect from a 'mechanic.'

The section in question was rotten, had been repaired before, but a new section would have cost nearly £100 since the section was about four feet long and had quite an involved shape. To fit it would have risked distorting the bodyshell. The repair cost about £5 worth of steel plate and about half a dozen hours of effort.

The chassis had rotted at the bottom of the U-section and had been repaired previously by welding a patch over the top of the rusty steel. I decided I had to cut all the rot away and get back to clean metal. The section is U-shaped and the bottom of the 'U' is the rusty part shown in the photograph. After removing underseal with a blowlamp and scraper I gave the section a going-over with a wire brush in the electric drill. This removed all the remaining underseal and some of the paint, leaving a cleaner surface to inspect.

I decided that the job would have to be

tackled in three steps. The first step was to replace the side of the 'U' shown in the photograph. The second step would be to replace the bottom of the 'U', with the third step being the replacement of the other side. The side not shown in the photograph is identical to the illustrated side.

You can see where I marked the side of the section with a pencil, to give a guide line for cutting. My front boundary is marked by the heavy strip of steel used to reinforce the spring mounting. You can see this in the photograph. Now I'll tell you what to do to tackle a similar job.

Take a sheet of cardboard and lay it over the rusty area. Mark with a pencil the shape of the side of the section. Remember that the top of the side is not straight, but curving. This will show up on your drawing. Now add half an inch to the top of the drawing to allow for a half inch lip. This lip will weld to the floor of the car.

When you have cut out a piece of card which fits exactly, lay the card on top of the panel steel. Scribe round the card with either a scriber or a pencil.

Cut out the steel with whatever method you have available to you. Tin snips are okay, but do not use the cutting torch. The resulting slag and distortion will ruin the patch panel before you finish cutting it out.

When you have the panel, mark on it the half inch lip which you will have to bend. Now this is where it gets tricky. If you have cut the curve out EXACTLY, then you will have little difficulty drawing a curved line half an inch in from the edge. Using the edge setter described in the second Chapter, bend the edge. Remember that the panel you have made is sided, that is it can only fit onto the car one way. If you turn it round it will not fit due to the curve. (The curve is not a constant radius).

Bend the edge OUT towards the outside of the car. When you have got the edge bent out using the edge setter, use the hammer and dolly to finish off the job. Constantly offer the panel up to the car as you go, so that you get a really good fit.

Once you have a good fit, you can turn your attention to the hole. This is not there by accident. It allows the channel to breathe and these holes are all too often blocked up with underseal.

Mark the location of the hole on your card template. Transfer the mark to the steel. Drill a small pilot hole. Next, using either a chassis punch or a tank cutter, make the hole the same size as on the original panel.

When you finish that, get the hammer and chisel out and remove ONLY that side of the section from the car. Leave the bottom and other side in situ.

Two new pieces of steel have been welded in place to restore the side and bottom of this chassis section. A new piece has still to be welded in on the other side of the Top Hat.

The complete job. A reinforcing piece fits over the main chassis section, and this has been remade in several parts. Look closely at the runs of weld which identify the different parts.

Clean up the ragged edges and again offer up your replacement panel. (By the way, now that you have removed a piece of chassis, don't sit in the car or put any heavy objects into the car. There is still a lot of strength in a chassis, even with one piece removed, but do not push your luck).

When everything fits, use suitable clamps and holding devices to fasten the panel in position. How did I do it? Okay, at the front end I used one of the Inter-grip clamps, while at the rear I used a 'G' clamp and a small piece of scrap steel. The new panel fitted at the top, at the front (due to the clamp), at the bottom (due to the original bottom section left in place) and at the rear (due to the 'G' clamp).

Make sure there is nothing to burn on the floor above the welding job. Get the torch out and put a couple of tack welds in place. If you have removed paint this will be an easy task. If not, you are making things difficult for yourself.

Once you have a couple of tacks in place (along the top, rear edge and front edge) weld the rest of the top and sides in position with a nice slow flame. You should be able to use a 1/16 inch welding rod for this. Do a good neat job.

When the side is welded in place, follow the same steps to make up the base. When you have the new base made up, cut out the old one. Again, if there are any holes in the bottom, you will have to reproduce these holes in your new panel. You may find it difficult to hold the bottom section in position. Try jacking it up! Use a jack and a small block of wood. Do up the jack until the wood just pushes the steel into position. I know it is sloping, but you should be able to do it. It only needs to hold until you get a tack weld in place.

Once again, once you have tacked, run weld round the three sides of the section (front, rear and one side).

When the bottom is in place, follow the original steps with a piece of card to make up the inner repair section. When you have your new side section made, cut out the old one from the car. By this time your neck is getting sore from lying under the car. Don't give up. Get the job finished and you can lie in the bath enthusing over a job well done!

Get some paint onto the repair as soon as you can, and when that is dry underseal it with a good heavy coat of bitumen.

Replacing Outriggers

The second repair job is more typical. It is a rusty outrigger, which is a short length of chassis section running from the main section out to the side of the car at the inner sill. This section attaches to the main chassis section, to the floor, and to the inner sill. Make sure all these areas are sound before trying to weld in a new outrigger.

If outriggers are not available for your car, don't give up. You can adapt something from another car, or make one from a length of Top Hat.

Once you have a replacement section, try it for fit under the car before cutting the old one away.

If your outrigger is from another car, and you are making the jacking hole, then it must be re-inforced with some extra steel. I used some heavy square-shaped washers which I found in a hardware shop. I think they are used in fencing jobs, where a bolt passes through a concrete fence post. A special washer is needed to spread the pull through the concrete. These washers were about 5 pence each and fairly heavily made.

This 1937 Chevrolet Coach shows a completely rusted-out floor but a basically sound main chassis. Anyone fancy restoring this sort of damage? Looks like the seat has seen better times, too! (Photo by Mark and Terry Hill).

Mark the location of the jacking hole and drill the hole in the top hat section. Hold it under the car to make sure it fits. Better still, use the actual jack to jack it gently into place. If all is well, remove the top hat chassis section and put the washer over the hole. You won't need to clamp it into position, just lay it over the hole. Make sure the two holes are the same size, otherwise you will have to drill the hole out after you weld.

With a number 2 or 3 tip in the torch, weld the washer onto the chassis section. As the two pieces of steel are different thicknesses, direct more of the heat onto the washer. You can get a nice neat job here, as you can do it in comfort, either on the ground or on the work bench.

This job builds up a lot of heat, so be careful about distortion. When the job cools enough, offer up the new section to see if it fits. If it is on the large side, don't worry, you can make adjustments quite easily. If however it is too short for the job, then you have made a mistake somewhere and must find another, more suitable section. You might be able to salvage the job by welding in bits of extra steel, but I want you to be in the position of knowing this beforehand (as part of the planning stage of the job) rather than create a salvage operation half way through.

Left, restoration has started on the instrument panel of this 1954 Studebaker Commander. Most of the rust on the transmission tunnel looks superficial and should clean up with a wire brush followed by a few coats of decent paint. Interesting use of the Mole-type clamp. Wish I had thought of that. (Photo by Mark and Terry Hill).

Below, a 1931 Essex, showing the wood rim wheels looking in a sorry state after 56 years. However, much of the steel-work looks quite sound. Cars were built with much heavier gauge steel in those days. (Photo by Mark and Terry Hill).

When you are happy with the fit of the new section, remove the old section. I use hammer and chisel again for this job. Once it's off clean up the area with wire brushes and grinders.

Locate the new section in position with either a screw jack or other suitable means. Make tack welds, check location again, then seam weld into position. (Seam welding will help to keep water out of the joins).

I've cut this description a bit short, but by now you should have the idea. Read all the other jobs described in the book and you will have a very good idea of what to do.

MacPherson Strut Towers

In this section I want to look at MacPherson strut towers, which were used on a lot of British Fords during the 1960s. They support the front suspension strut and have a nasty habit of rusting-out near the top. Many Fords of this period have had the tops plated in order to pass the Ministry of Transport annual test. However, to do a proper restoration you should consider replacing the rusty parts and fitting new ones. This is quite cheap to do (currently around £10 to £15 per side) but takes a little bit of know-how to get right.

As you can see from the photographs, the whole engine bay looks much better if there are no unsightly welds to be seen.

As with other jobs described in this book, spend some time with a screwdriver prodding the rusty area to find the extent of the damage.

The assembly consists of four main parts. There is a top patch plate, which you can get away with if the corrosion is not too severe. The lower three pieces go underneath the wing and attach to the inner wing. Normally the top plate, and the round, lower plate have three holes drilled which helps the locating process a great deal.

Once you have discovered the extent of the rust, decide if you need the upper plate or all four pieces. When you decide, remember that this is a fairly big operation to carry out, especially if the wing is still on the car. It means you are working for a lot of the time up inside a wing, so you will need a source of light.

The first time I tackled this job I made up the pan (the round steel part at the top of the assembly, under tha wing) from bits of steel. Its hard work cutting out a hole that size. Later I discovered the parts were available, so the second time I did it, things went better.

Again, I don't want to waste time covering mechanical items already described in lots of manuals. So, remove the suspension strut from its top mounting and give yourself room to work. Remove the bonnet too, as this will let light into the job, and stop you banging your head every five minutes! Examine the top pan closely, and decide if it needs to be replaced. Although you have to buy a 'kit' with the pan and two vertical members, there is no rule which says that you must use all of it. If the pan is sound, and I mean completely sound, then leave it alone. It is unlikely that the verticals will have rusted except near the top, so have a close look at this area.

I'll assume that your pan is rusty and that you are going to replace both pan and verticals. Start by cleaning off any underseal over the joint between the vertical and the inner wing. When you find the join, start to cut the spot welds with hammer and chisel. As you have your head under the wing to do this, don't make matters more difficult than they have to be. Do a neat cut, otherwise you will have to spend extra time repairing the damage you inflicted.

Cut one vertical off at a time. You should find you are leaving a nice line of dull paint where the inner wing was covered by the vertical. This will serve as your replacing line. If you are worried, mark the line with pencil or marker pen.

Detach the vertical from the pan with hammer and chisel. Repeat the process for the second vertical. When both are off, turn your attention to the pan.

The problem here is getting your chisel in between the pan and the upper, inner wing. Although I always advocate a four inch chisel, this is one time when you will

A typical MacPherson strut tower, showing two vertical supporting members welded to the inner wing, plus a round pan at the top to locate the MacPherson strut mounting. Repairs can be done quite cheaply.

A Cortina rear chassis repair section, clearly showing the reinforcing built into the spring mounting area. I have adapted several of these sections to use as front outriggers on my Cortinas. (Incidentally, the correct front outriggers are still available).

find it difficult to use a four inch, due to space restrictions.

Try breaking the welds from underneath the wing. You should be able to start off like this, then move to the top of the car and put the chisel into the mounting hole at an angle, and break some more welds. You may find that the lower edge of the pan is welded to the inner wing, so be prepared to look at that area if the pan does not come away easily.

Once it is all off, clean up the pan area with a wire brush and grinding stone. If all the hammering has shown up any more rust, decide if you need to make that good before fitting the new pan.

Having cleaned all the surface underneath the inner wing where the pan goes, bolt the new pan in position with three nuts and bolts. Use bolts which are a snug fit in the holes, as this will increase your accuracy in locating the pan.

Remember that this pan and vertical kit is 'handed', that is, a kit for the driver's side won't fit the passenger's side. Don't try and fit the wrong pan.

When the pan is located, weld it in position. How? Good question. I welded the inside of the big hole (where the top of the strut goes) to the edge of the inner wing. In other words, I melted the edge of the inner wing into the edge of the pan.

Underneath, I welded the bottom edge of the pan at the point where it met the inner wing. Next, the verticals.

You need two or three clamps for this job. On my verticals there were a couple of small holes, used I presume, during the manufacturing process. You could drill through these holes, into the inner wing and bolt the vertical in position. This, and a couple of clamps — one of which has to be between the pan and the vertical, allows you to locate the vertical.

Once its in place, and thoroughly checked for accuracy of position, put some tack welds on. Check again, then run your final welds. I did not seam weld this job. I probably should have done, but instead I ran an inch or so of weld, skipped an inch or two, then repeated the welding. The bits not welded were hammered down to prevent water entering, and after three years have given no problems.

Repeat for the second vertical. There are no particular problems with this job, but you may find it daunting. I did both sides in a weekend, but on reflection probably should have taken a bit longer.

Top Plate

If your rust is confined to the top of the strut, then you can fit a suspension top plate, which is a repair patch which goes over the top of the inner wing. Depending

Don't let mechanical items get in your way — move 'em! There are plenty of workshop manuals available which cover all the mechanical dismantling. This MacPherson strut is disconnected at the top to allow work on the top of the strut tower.

I was lucky on this car — it did not need much work on the MacPherson strut towers. You can see the front chassis repair, the front panel repair, inner sill repair, and main chassis repair.

on the car, it can run back to the bulkhead, or just cover the area round the strut. I don't want to go into a lot of detail on this one. Treat it as a patch and don't weld it over the top of rusty steel. You are wasting

your time if you do.

Follow these steps for fitting a top plate:

Clean off the entire area and inspect for rust. Clean off any loose rust and treat any

You can see the much heavier chassis members on this light commercial van. It takes a lot of rust to eat into this thickness of steel, so this one has probably been scrapped due to mechanical problems.

areas of surface rust. If you have extensive problems consider removing the top of the inner wing and using the patch as a new top.

Remove the three strut top bolts. Bolt the new strut top in place with the three bolts.

Tap round the edges of the top plate to get a good fit with the inner wing. Put some tack welds in position.

Take care not to burn any wiring looms, or plastic windscreen washer bottles or pipes. Look out for the Control Box if this is mounted on the inner wing.

Once you have half a dozen tack welds in position, seam weld all round. This will involve welding the patch near the rear bulkhead. Be very careful, as you can set fire to trim, carpets and the whole car, if you ignite anything inside the car when welding in this area. I can't over-emphasise the danger in this area. Be very careful.

The edge of the patch will also have to be welded to the edge of the outer wing. This can damage paintwork if not done carefully, so this job should not be considered a five-minute fix.

This Morris Minor changed hands recently for about £300. It has had some welding work done underneath and looks very smart, but the owner decided it was time to part company. If looked after properly this sort of 'durable' car could last for ever.

Take your time and get a neat result, otherwise you will be ashamed to open the bonnet at the next club meeting. Take a pride in your metalwork and remember, anyone who can do decent chassis repairs has learnt a rare skill.

Remember to apply paint as soon as you have finished the welding work. Don't leave it until the next day or you will find that rust has started to appear on the surface. Get some heavy coats of underseal or protective paint on NOW.

Captive Nuts

Very often you will find that a panel has a captive nut attached to it. By 'captive nut' I mean a nut which is attached to a panel, usually by weld or braze. It is used to attach the panel to another assembly, or fix something to the panel. If you need to fix a nut to a panel you are repairing there are several ways to tackle the job.

You can fix any size nut to a panel quite simple. First decide (accurately) where you want the nut to go. Mark the centre of it with a scriber or sharp point. Drill a suitable clearance hole for the bolt being used. Now fix the nut over the hole by using the bolt and a couple of washers. Once everything is in place you can braze the nut in position. Brazing is normally quite strong enough for this sort of job, but if you want you can weld the nut. It takes a lot of heat to get a nut hot enough to weld, and you have to take care not to distort or burn the parent panel. Yet again, I say try it out on a piece of scrap.

Unusual Clamps

Don't be afraid to try an unusual method of fixing panels together before welding them. In a narrow lock-up garage I have used a piece of wood wedged between the wall and the inner wing to hold a patch panel against an inner wing. It takes a couple of attempts to get the patch panel exactly where you want it, but it can be done. As soon as you have it in place, get a couple of tack welds onto it to secure it. After that its easy!

Chassis Misalignment

On older cars with separate chassis or frames, the need often arises to check if the frame is bent or otherwise distorted. Although this does not strictly fall with the subject of Panel Craft, I want to quickly explain what is involved.

Find a flat, repeat flat level surface. A concret garage floor will be suitable if it is exaclty flat. If there are depressions in the floor then you are not going to get accurate measurements. Using four screw jacks, place the chassis on the jacks and raise it about fifteen inches from the floor. Make sure the chassis is flat, use a spirit level if necessary.

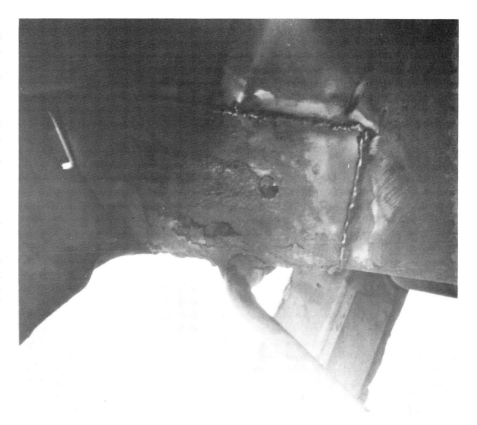

The front chassis member of this Cortina has already been repaired but the rot has eaten through again. Often, new patches are just welded on top of the old ones. I had to cut all this away and fit an entirely new patch.

Nasty looking corrosion round the main chassis, next to the front outrigger. This car was originally very well protected with underseal, otherwise it would not have survived so long. Even so, it needed a lot of work to revive it.

First measure from a number of points on one side of the chassis and the same points on the other side of the chassis to the floor. If the chassis if lying flat, then all the measurements between similar points to the floor should be the same, or within one eighth of an inch. For example if you measure from the lower edge of the frame just in front of a certain mounting hole, then that distance to the floor should be the same as from the same point on the other side of the frame to the floor. If your measurements show a difference of about one eighth of an inch, seek professional help. You have a distorted frame which must be repaired. Rectification work can be done and need not be too costly if you can do all the stripping and assembly work yourself.

Another test involves diagonal measurements. Use a piece of thin string and a pointed weight, such as a plumb-bob pointer. Locate the string at various points on the chassis — wherever there is a similar point on the opposite side. Points to use are the very front edge of the chassis, spring mountings, body mounting points etc. Mark each point where the plumb-bob touches the floor. You need to have eight such points, four on each side.

When all eight points are plotted on the floor, draw lines between a point on one side and the next point on the other side. Measure the length of these diagonal lines. If any diagonal is longer or shorter than the opposite diagonal linking the same points, then the frame is misaligned. Again the figure of an eighth of an inch is a fair guide to the straightness of the frame. Any more than that, and you should go to a professional.

Similar tests can be performed on modern monocoque or unibody cars. But remember, if you suspect major, or accident damage has distorted the frame or chassis it is dangerous and irresponsible not to have it rectified professionally.

Access

One of the biggest problems about chassis repairing is actually getting access to the problem area. Ramps or a pit can help but these both have drawbacks. Welding down a pit without anyone above watching for trouble can be extremely dangerous, as any fire starting will be well alight before you can get back up to the floor again. Ramps are easier to manage and much cheaper, but they don't give you the height you want. You always want more height when chassis welding!

The best solution, although an expensive one is a device which rotates the car. This allows the chassis to be brought to a suitable working level, while allowing the car to rolled back to its normal position when required.

These roller devices cost between £400 and £500 but you may want to consider buying one if you have long term plans to restore a number of cars. Alternatively, you may be able to hire one.

Most people are going to have to make do with axle stands, so their welding is going to be done from a lying position. This puts considerable strain on various parts of the body, but especially the neck. Try to get a cushion or an old overall to support your neck. Also, if you do feel a strain while welding, stop and come up for a breath of fresh air. You will actually help the job by stopping every so often, as you are not building up lots of heat to cause distortion.

I hope I have given you some ideas about chassis welding. There is a lot you can do, and as I said before people are put-off by the mention of chassis repairs, so you can buy some real bargain cars.

In the next Chapter I will show you how to repair and replace floor sections so well you won't know where you did the repair in a few months time!

Inspection pits can be very useful for working under cars. This little pit is about five feet, six inches deep and cost me around £150 to build, (plus a lot of digging!).

This Wolseley Six Eighty from the 1950s features a monocoque bodyshell, known then as mono-construction. Note the distinctive bell mounted above the front bumper, and the roof mounted aerial of this British Police version.

Below, all the Cortina chassis work mentioned in this book applies to the Ford Corsair as well. Often overlooked, these very distinctive cars can be restored on a budget to provide reliable drive to work motoring. This later model, photographed at Hagley Hall, has the V4 engine.

Floor Pans

This Morris Minor bodyshell has been rotated so that work can be done on the underside. Although it does not look particularly bad, this shell will probably need work on the floor panels, just below the exhaust pipe. (Photo by Roger Turner.)

Very often your restoration project will require work on the floors. This is often the first rust that you notice as soon as you lift the carpets to find out why your feet are getting wet! In this Chapter we will have a look at rusty floors, and what can be done to put matters right.

Water can enter from numerous places, such as through the felt seal along the middle of the door, from holes caused by rust, from man-made holes such as aerials or mirrors and of course through the windscreen rubber seal.

The first thing to do is lift the carpets and any underfelt which may be there. This will allow you to form a better idea of the extent of the damage. Clean up as much wetness as you can with rags. It helps if you remove any rubbish such as cigarette ends and chewing gum wrappers.

If the car is a restoration project and is going to be off the road for some time, take the seats out altogether, even for an inspection. Use a screwdriver to poke and prod

all over the floor. A little experience of this will allow you to notice the different sound a rusty panel makes. If you dried off the floor as I suggested in the last paragraph, it may now help if you scour the floor with a wire brush. You can use a hand brush but if you have an electric drill then so much the better. This will allow you to see if there is any loose flaky rust which will show that there has been a problem for some time. Of course, if big chunks of the floor come away in your hand, you should have known about it when you bought the car.

Rot generally follows a similar pattern on similar vehicles. Have a look at the Cortina rebuild at the end of the book. This will give you a good idea of where to look for rust in a monocoque-type bodyshell. You may have a large area of rusty steel which has lots of small holes. This is probably the sign of a wet carpet holding water. Unless you can clean and fill each hole, you will have to treat this problem as a large section of floor to replace.

If you have medium sized holes in certain areas, these probably occur where two or more steel sections join. Water has penetrated the join and spread outwards as corrosion. In this sort of situation you will have to repair or replace the adjacent panels as well as the floor panel.

NOW is the time to discover the size and extent of the problem – not after you have spent an hour welding in a new floor section, then find you need another new piece of steel. Take time over this stage and get it right – first time.

Answer these questions:

1) Is the rust confined to one section (such as a floor panel?)

2) Does the rust extend to other adjacent sections?

3) What make and model of car is it ? (Is it a common model or a less-popular one?)

4) Are new floor panels available from either the Main Dealer or a specialist supplier?

'Ere, shouldn't there be a floor in this car, mate? The Cortina driver's side floor panel removed, ready for a trial fitting of the new Escort floor panel. This panel provides a nice cheap repair. Most of the rubbish on the garage floor is the old panel!

5) Are the other rusty panels available too?

6) Are you confident about tackling the job?

When you have positive answers to all these questions, you can plan your next move.

You might be thinking, this is all very interesting but why don't I just put down this book, get the welding torch out and get started! PLEASE DON'T. From experience, I have found that this is the stage that the job gets spoilt. Plan it out and the end result will be neater, and the satisfaction that much greater.

Once you have a good idea of what is involved, decide if the best action is replace or patch. Both methods are acceptable, provided that the welding is satisfactory.

In the Cortina shown in the photo, the rust was in patches over the drivers floor. Once I marked out the affected area it was clear that it should be replaced, rather than patched. There are no floor sections available from Ford for a 23 year old car, so I began to look through the body parts catalogues I had collected.

It pays to look at other cars from the same manufacturer first to see if something will fit. Very often this is the case, with one model sharing a design idea with other later models. Eventually, I decided that the Ford Escort off-side floor panel looked as though it might fit. I went to the nearest dealer and asked to see an Escort panel. I had the measurements from the Cortina's rusty floor with me and after comparing the measurements against the Escort panel, decided that it could be made to fit. In actual fact it was a good few inches larger all round, so I was confident that it would fit, and at less that £5 it seemed a fairly safe bet. Good value for an extra 20 years motoring!

When I got home I made a final check to ensure that the panel would fit, by laying it over the area it was intended to replace. It looked good.

Before starting to cut out the old floor, I made a final check both above and below the floor to make sure that I had found all the rust. When this is done and you have marked out the rusty area, start to cut metal. I used a hammer and chisel for most of the floor as it provides a quick and reasonably clean cut. I tried to cut within the marked area so that I could trim the edges later with the grinder or tin snips. You will find that the floor panel is spot welded to the front chassis outrigger which also forms the front jacking point. This was a problem on all three of my cars, as they were pretty rotten and needed replacing.

An LMC Panels Escort floor panel which can be adapted to fit the Cortina MKI. It needs a bit of modification, but makes a neat repair, and is readily available.

In this example I want to deal with each job separately, so I'll carry on as though we are only replacing the floor panel. It is better to do one job at a time anyway, but as I know the model quite well I decided I could cut out the chassis member and the floor at the same time.

What you end up with on the garage floor is frightening! There is a pile of rusty steel and an even bigger pile of dirt and debris from the chassis section. Once you have the old floor panels cut out, it pays to sweep the floor. One very good reason for doing this is that if there are any small splinters of metal left over from the chiselling, you won't find them with your knees!

Right, old floor cut out, and you're ready to offer the new panel to the 'hole.' You may find, as I did that the new floor panel is not flat. What I mean is that the edges may raised slightly in relation to the rest of the panel. The thing to do here is get a hammer and dolly and flatten the edges.

You may also find, as I did, that the floor panel is a little too large. In fact I found I could rotate my floor panel and use the 'side edge' of the panel as my front edge. The only problem was that a groove had been formed in the new floor panel and this got in the way of the chassis section.

Some more exercise with the hammer and dolly flattened the groove at the offending point.

The edges of my panel were a little too large, so they were trimmed and bent to fit. I also formed a small (half inch) lip on the edge of the floor panel where it meets the inner sill. Once everything was adjusted and encouraged to fit, I offered it up again to the hole.

When you are satisfied that things are looking good, make a final check for fire hazards, then get the welding torch ready. I use a number one tip for this sort of work and I always seam weld — right round the floor panel.

Some people just braze, or run short lengths of weld but I reckon to try to do this sort of job properly and weld it. In one American magazine I saw an article which showed the 'restorer' fitting a sheet of steel which once saw service as the side of a battleship. He cut this out to shape, and brazed it over the old rusty floor! I don't want you to try anything like that. Do the job properly. Once its done you can forget it for a long time!

First make a few tack welds along each side of the panel. Once these are in place, check to confirm that the panel is exactly where you want it to be, and that the edges of the floor panel are straight. Don't worry if you have to hammer them occasionally during the welding process. This will help to ensure a better finish to the job.

I like to 'leapfrog' around this type of repair. This stops a build-up of heat in one area and avoids distortion. I recommend you weld an inch or so, then move the torch to another point, and weld another few inches. In this way you can move round the panel and see the job progressing. Its important for the newcomer to metalwork to see the job progressing, otherwise he gets disappointed and either rushes the job to finish it, or abandons the project altogether.

Take your time, and get it right!

One word of warning when leapfrogging. Don't move along the panel and kneel or sit on the bit you have just welded. Don't laugh. It happens all the time!

When you have completed the welding on the floor panel, drill any new holes that you have to make, such as for seat mountings, seat belt mountings and so on. Seat belt mountings MUST be reinforced with a large steel washer, and these are usually sold with the seat belt kit.

Remember if you have to weld a nut underneath the floor there are several ways to do this without lying underneath. For example, you can weld the nut to a small square of scrap steel. Then drill a hole in the floor where the bolt is to go, plus a couple of other, smaller holes close by. This allows you to plug weld from the top. Plug welding is fully described in another Chapter.

In the photographs of the Morris Minor, the whole floor panel has been replaced with a new one. This is not too difficult to do, especially if you have the device shown, which allows you to 'roll' a car on its side.

Remember that the larger areas of floor are often supported by a chassis outrigger. Sometimes these outriggers end in jacking points, so you will have to ensure that they are sound. The penalty is to have a flat tyre and screw your jack right up through the sill and floor! Don't let it happen to you.

Boot Floors

Once you have sorted out the driver and passenger floors, its time to turn your attention to the boot floor. This includes the spare wheel well, and if you are as lucky with cars as I seem to be, you will have some work to do!

Once again, lift any mats or carpets. In fact don't mess around, just take them out altogether and spread them on the ground to dry if weather permits. Now get that trusty screwdriver and have a prod

The Escort floor pan being tried for size against the Cortina floor. Note the cut-out in the floor panel for the 'lump' in the Cortina floor on which the seat mounts. Work has also been done on the bottom of the A Post.

around. Try not to stick the screwdriver through the petrol tank top if it forms part of the boot floor. You will probably find rust in a couple of areas. The spare wheel well will probably be pretty rotten, as water tends to gather there. On the opposite side of the boot, there may be a flat panel instead of a spare wheel well. Its not uncommon for this to be rotten too, as the photograph shows. Don't give up yet.

If you car has a spare wheel well, where the wheel lies flat, there will probably be extensive rust where water has gathered. If there is water there, allow it to drain away. Very often there is a rubber bung somewhere in the well designed to let water drain away. You may even find it has a hole in it — once you clear away the debris and bits of soggy paper.

Pay attention to the areas where the chassis

attaches to the boot floor. Or to put it another way, where the boot floor attaches to the chassis. (Often if you think of these things in a different way, they can help you to do the job more easily).

If you find you have work to do in the boot area, your next problem is the petrol tank. To remove or not to remove?

If the car is a stripped out bodyshell, then the answer is obvious. If the tank is not out, then take it out.

If however the car is being restored at week-ends and you drive it to work during the week, you have a tricky problem. If you are absolutely sure that you will get too close to the tank, leave it in place. However, if you are worried about how close you might be, then take it out.

Having taken the tank out, don't be

tempted to weld until any petrol spills have been mopped up and covered in sand.

On my last restoration I had to replace the right hand side of the boot floor, fabricate the double skin section under it, make up a new floor over the top of the rear chassis leg, weld in a new chassis leg and fabricate a new spare wheel well from sheet steel. This took several weekends and evenings. I am always amazed when people tell me how long they took to do a job. I always seem to take five times longer. However, I'm working on the basis that I'll be keeping the car for a long time, while they seem to sell their's pretty quickly.

Let's run through the above list of jobs. The first one I tackled was to replace the right hand side of the boot floot. Luckily I found an as-new panel in a local scrap yard for about £5. Ten minutes with hammer and chisel soon had it out. There was a tiny little rust spot at one corner, but overall it was in great shape. If you can't get a second-hand one, then a look in the address section at the end of this book should help. I'll bet you can find what you need within three telephone calls! If you are absolutely stuck, read the end of this Chapter where I give some pointers to making your own floor sections from a flat sheet of steel!

The Escort floor panel welded in position. You can clearly see where the weld was run. After a good clean up and some paint, you will never know it has been replaced.

Don't think of car dismantlers as sources of mechanical spares only. Look at all those body panels, doors etc, on display in this yard. Watch out for the dog, though! This type of yard always has one at least.

This same panel is fitted to several Fords, including Cortina, Capri and Classic. The old rusty one I hacked out is photographed so that you can see how bad it was.

On the left hand edge of the panel is a half inch, 90 degree lip, where it joins to the next panel. Some of this joining edge was missing from my car, so I had to fit the new boot floor panel, then fabricate some new steel to join to it.

This took just a few hours, but I still had the problem of making up a new double skin section underneath. I left that till later, as I wanted to see some progress in the boot.

Next I turned my attention to the spare wheel well. This needed a new side and new bottom. I measure up and decided I would make the bottom in three pieces, and the side in two pieces. I cut out the two new side pieces first and measured them against the rusty ones. A few final trims and I was ready to remove the old side pieces. This was done with hammer and chisel, but its not easy, as half the time you need to be underneath the car, and the other half you are lying over the boot.

A couple of clamps held the wheel well sides in position, and I arranged the two repair pieces to butt together. After some tack welds, I removed the clamps and

This is the old boot floor panel which I removed from 'CAN' during restoration. Luckily, I got an as-new panel from a scrap car.

The passenger side floor this time, and a smaller welding job. Here the rust damaged area is being removed with hammer and chisel. This type of damage can be repaired cheaply with a sheet of steel as shown over the page.

All this repair is, is a piece of steel with a 90 degree lip at the left side. This lip is welded to the edge of the inner sill. The Inter-grip clamps keep everything in place during tack welding.

Try jacking up this Morris Minor with that rusty jacking point. The whole chassis section looks a bit suspect, so a replacement is the only answer. Some floor panel work is needed too. (Photo by Roger Turner).

What a nice neat job. This is the new chassis outrigger and jacking point fitted on the Morris Minor. It is the opposite side of the car to the previous photograph, but you can clearly see the shiny new steel.

seam welded the pieces in place. So far so good.

Next, I cut out the old bottom of the wheel well in a single large chunk. This allowed me to use the rusty bit as a template if I got into difficulties later. I divided the bottom into three pieces and made a cardboard template for my first piece. It consists of a flat sheet, with a half inch lip on the side where it meets the well side. I had to cut some 'V's in this lip, to allow the sheet to be bent to the well floor contours. This was quite easy to do, and my first attempt was acceptable. I then cut this out of steel. This too fitted nicely, so I tacked it into position. The well was starting to look better already.

In the next session a few nights later, I welded in the first and second sections of the well floor. Right at the deepest part of the well there should be a drain hole, so I drilled a pilot hole, then cut a decent sized hole with my chassis punch. When the job is complete, and the well painted, I will fit a rubber grommet to the hole.

I began to realise that the final section, which blends into the rear of the wheel arch was going to need some extra time on

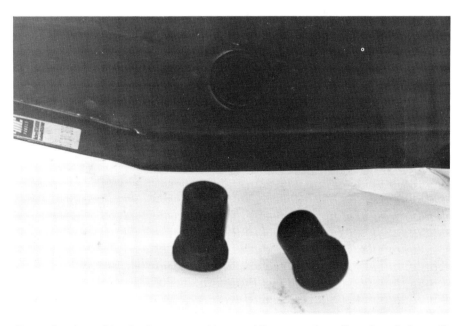

Remember that rubber bushes are used to mount the rear springs. If you have to burn off an old chassis section, don't burn your bushes!

it to get the shape right. I decided to leave that and go onto the chassis leg at the other side. Also, my back was complaining

about having to bend over into the boot when I was welding!

LEG SURGERY

This is one of the most common replacement jobs on a monocoque car, replacing the rusty end of a chassis section. Luckily there are several manufacturers making repair section, and they cost less than £10.

I carefully measured the replacement chassis section, then compared the measurement on the existing section. I measure again and marked my cutting line.

For this job you have to remove the rear spring hanger. This involves releasing two bolts which may be tightly rusted in place. Heat from the welding torch soon shifted them and the shackle was knocked out. (I am skipping over a lot of the mechanical details here, as there are about a dozen manuals available for the Cortina alone. Refer to any one of them for the mechanical work). If you use heat to release the rear spring hanger bolts, remember that you might damage the rubber bushes. I intended to replace these bushes anyway, but you may plan to refit yours. Don't burn 'em up, as they smell awful!

Following that I had to use heat again to release the two bolts which bolt the bumper-bar bracket onto the end of the chassis section. Once they were heated they came off easily but protested noisily.

I next chiselled the chassis section away from the boot floor. As I mentioned earlier, the floor in this area needed repairs, so I was not too careful about getting the old section out.

I admit I used the welding torch to cut part of the section as it proved a little more robust than I had expected. Once it was off, I cleaned up the remaining steel with a grinding stone in the electric drill.

Next I trial fitted the replacement section. This fitted well, with just some minor adjustements needed at the front of the repair section. I like to try to overlap this type of join, so I cut little slots about half an inch long in the existing chassis, so that the top hat would bend open and allow the new section to slot inside. This sounds fairly easy but I can assusre you it is a bit of a fiddle, especially when you are lying on the ground to do it.

Once this was located properly, I put in the bumper-bar bolts, which bolt into the end piece on the chassis section. This helps to locate the part properly prior to welding.

With one final check to see that the top hat section actually met the floor (a few taps with a hammer soon sorted that out) I was ready to tack weld.

I tacked on both sides of the chassis section, and at front and rear. After one final check to ensure that everything is still where it should be, I seam welded the section into place, leapfrogging around the

You are looking into the spare wheel well of a MKI Cortina. This sort of rust damage is typical, but can be repaired. New sections are also available if you choose to buy rather than make.

section so that I would not cause too much distortion. I have done this same job at least a dozen times before on various cars, so I knew what to expect. If you are doing it for the first time, allow plenty of time, as it is a real pain in the neck lying on your side welding above your head.

Try resting your head against a spare wheel. This gives some relief, but if you are hurting, take the job in smaller stages. You'll get there!

Once the chassis section was in place, I next patched the boot floor. This involved cutting two or three pieces of steel plate, and forming a half inch lip on one side. This lip mates up with the lip on the boot floor section which I had replaced earlier.

Once these were tacked in place, I seam welded the angle-joint formed by the two lips meeting. This is done from underneath, but is reasonably easy to do. I then finished welding the pieces together from the top. If you are very energetic, you can sit in the boot to do this, but as I mentioned before, don't kneel on the bit you just welded...

Right, just to recap. I have fitted two of the three spare wheel well repair sections. I have fitted a new chassis leg, fitted a new right hand side boot floor panel, and repaired the boot floor adjacent to this panel. The only thing left to do now is finish the spare wheel well.

The final section which had been causing

me a bit of a problem is the one which joins to the inner wheel arch. I probably fell into the old trap of using steel which was too heavy, so I now had difficulty shaping it to suit.

I had to make a few cuts in the edge of the patch to get it to bend to shape, but after a bit of swearing it fell into place. A few tack welds ensured it would not escape! I then seam welded round the final patch, fixing it to the middle of the three sections fitted.

There is one other job to do, which I have not mentioned. The spare wheel well sides, and the three well bottom sections have not yet been joined. Although I am mentioning this last, I actually did the welding after I fitted each bottom section. Just clamp the lower edge of the side, and the half inch lip on the bottom, and weld them together. This pulls the whole assembly together, and suddenly you have a new spare wheel well.

Because I had done all this work over a period of a few weeks, I went over everything with a wire brush in the electric drill, to clean any surface rust off. A good heavy coat of rustproofing primer went on, followed by another thinner coat later.

Although the whole job took a few weeks, I reckon it will last another 20 years at least. Just to round off this Chapter on floors, let's have a look at making your own floor section from a piece of steel.

Double Skin

Underneath the new right hand side boot floor section is another sheet of steel which is joined to the outer corner panel to form a double skin. This bit usually rots away, as it had done on my cars, so the only thing to do is make up a replacement. I use a card-

The ex-Roger Clark Cortina again, and an immaculate boot area. Note the battery in the right hand side, and that simple device for locating spare wheels! The steel tube across the boot is used to mount the petrol tank.

board template and make the sheet up in two pieces. On the lower edge you need a half inch lip again, and this needs to be formed at an angle, so that it fits inside the outer panel's lip. This may sound complicated, but as soon as you look at the panels on your car you will see the problem.

Once the two pieces are welded in place, I drilled a hole in the new inner skin so that I could spray some protection into the cavity.

This double skin replacement is a bit of a fiddle and it took me longer than expected, but one of the reasons is that everything had to be done from underneath the car. This discomfort adds considerably to your time.

Making a Floor

You need accurate measurements, and a few basic tools to make your own floor section. Let's start with accurate measurements.

You need to measure exactly to extent of the new section you want to make. 'Near enough' is no good. Measure twice, or three times, the old floor section. (This is why I say, never throw away a section until the new one is made and fitted correctly. There is a lot of information locked up in a scrap section!)

Mark out your measurements on a piece of steel. Do NOT cut this out yet. Because you are going to hammer some grooves in

Cortina Estates have different boot floors to the saloon. All the body drawings are reproduced in the Cortina Restoration section towards the end of the book. This nice example shows the distinctive wood panels on the side of the bodywork.

Repairs completed on the inner wheel arch and floor pan of this Capri. The patching has been done in four pieces. The job has been given some paint to protect it and will soon be coated with underseal as well. I did this repair a few years ago, and reckon I could do the job better today! You do get much neater over the years...

Front view of the Mercury pick-up. Note the sturdy frame sections at the front which have to support the weight of the Chevrolet motor. Suspension is believed to be from a Corvette. This enthusiast is lucky – he has a nice big workshop! (Photo Mark and Terry Hill.)

Interior view of a 1949 Mercury pick-up, showing lots of activity on the chassis frame and floor pan. New floor panels will be fitted to the angle-iron frame to provide a strong floor. Seat supports and seat belt anchor points must be planned into a job like this. (Photo Mark and Terry Hill.)

The Capri again, this time repairs are still being made to the driver's side, rear inner wheel arch and floor panels. The wheel arch has already had major surgery, but the scars will fade when paint is applied.

Left. The rear frame of the Mercury pick-up. Heavy steel sections form the new frame, and the welder has made a good job of finishing off all the joins. All the surface rust will be cleaned off before paint is applied. This sort of frame should last for ever if properly painted. (Photo Mark and Terry Hill.)

Right. General view of the Mercury pick-up. The rear frame is new, and is joined to the original frame just behind the cab. Don't tackle anything like this until you are confident about your metalwork. This job looks like it will be a real winner when completed. (Photo Mark and Terry Hill.)

the floor to make it look like an original floor panel, you will have to allow some extra steel. Mark out where the grooves are to run, taking the measurements from the old section. If you have thrown the old bit away, try looking at the same floor section on the other side of the car.

Mark lines on the steel where you want the groove to run. Remember to mark which way the grooves are to run. What I mean is, do the grooves run in the steel so that they bulge downwards, below the level of the floor, or as is so often the case, do they bulge upwards, forming ridges in the floor. If they point upwards, then you will have to hammer from the 'underneath'. Get this sorted out in your mind before you start hammering!

When all this is marked out, and you have allowed a safety margin for your measurements, start to work the steel.

If you are using a grooved, or 'shrinking dolly' start to form the grooves. Take them gently, a bit at a time. You may find the steel is starting to distort. One way to overcome this is to form a lip along one edge. This may be the joining lip for the floor section. You can make this lip first, as long as you are not going to 'groove' withing a couple of inches of the lip. The lip will help to keep the section in shape.

Continue making the grooves until you are happy with them. On the boot floor section for the Cortina, which we discussed earlier in the Chapter, the grooves are not straight. Some of them curve on the surface of the steel. This is not too difficult to copy.

If you think things are getting too difficult for you, stop grooving and use what you have made. Because you have made grooves, you will have distorted the measurements you marked down originally. Check and double check the measurements and mark new ones on the floor section. Cut it out, making sure you follow the correct set of measurements. If you don't, then start again!

Once again, don't get put off by the half finished job. Once your floor panel is welded in place, painted, then undersealed, you will be pleased as punch. The only thing is, because it is a floor section, it's down there but no-one ever looks, so only you can take a pride in it! You could always take some photographs...

I hope I have given you some ideas about floor repairs. They need not be too difficult, and with a bit of flair you can produce really exciting results. In the next Chapter I'll show you how to 'section' body panels to create neat, tidy repairs which won't cost you a fortune.

A really nice example of the early Ford Anglia. This one carries quite a rare A registration and is in excellent condition. The photo was taken in a Motorway services area, so don't think these 'older' cars are not useful on long trips.

The area behind the passenger seat of the Ford Capri. All repairs completed, the floor area has been painted and in this photo has just received a nice heavy coat of shiny black underseal. Next job, fit the carpets!

Sectioning And Patching

A 1954 Studebaker Commander at the start of restoration. Only a few thousand examples of this model were built. There is a lot of rust damage on the front wing, just in front of the driver's door. A lot of the surface rust on other panels is caused by bird droppings. (Photo by Terry Hill.)

In the first part of this Chapter, I want to look at a technique known as 'sectioning.' As its name suggests, you use a section or part of one panel to repair another panel. Very often the section is not a complete panel, as part of a panel can be used on two different jobs. This situation could arise where new panels are very scarce, and it could be justified on a cost basis.

This technique attracts bad publicity from time to time, as someone welds the halves of two different cars together and tries to pass it off as new! This *can* be done but it has to be done very carefully, and the end result has to justify the time and expense of doing it. I'm not suggesting that you start off doing something like this. Let's keep things simple, and you will still achieve good results.

Say, for example, that your car needs a new door skin. Let's also suppose that there are no door skins available — at any price. You could have one made by a professional, but there is a cheaper alternative. Usually doors rust out at the bottom. So why not 'section-in' a new bottom half of the door?

Similarly, if the front of your wing rusts out, why replace the whole wing? You can buy replacement front wing sections for many cars, and I don't doubt that some of these sections can be adapted to fit other cars from the same manufacturer. As we will also see later in the Chapter, you can make up your own sections to achieve a cheap, effective repair.

Let's have a close look at a sectioning job.

Front Valance Patching

The front valance of a car takes a bit of a beating over the years. What with rust, flying stones, salt and the occasional parking bump, it can look a bit sorry for its self. I reckoned I could save the entire front panel of my £25 Cortina by piecing in a new section of steel at either side. This steel patch would run the full height of the valance, from the bottom, to the line where it meets the chrome grill. The curve is gentle and it is only at the outside edge that the curve gets a bit complicated. As things turned out, I had to fabricate a lot of the driver's side of the front panel, below the headlamp, as well.

Firstly, I marked off the area to be removed on the front panel. I allowed a little bit extra for possible hidden rust, and after marking with a pencil, I cut the old section out with tin snips. Standing looking at the front panel, I now began to wonder if I had done the right thing! This feeling soon passed as I cut out a cardboard template for the new patch. As you will see in the Cortina Restoration feature, I did this job on both sides of the car. However, the side which still had the wing on was much easier to do, as I had an extra reference point.

After a couple of trial runs with various bits of cardboard, I got the shape right. Next, I transferred the shape onto steel. Remember not to use steel which is too thick. I made this error as I had nothing else available at the time. It turned out that my choice was not too far out, but a lighter gauge of steel would have made the job a little bit easier.

Once the steel patch was cut out, I tried it for fit. Not too bad. It needed a few adjustments to get the curve right, but that did not take long. Basically, I bent the patch on my knee until it was right! Once I was sure it was a good fit, I attached a couple of Inter-grip welding clamps to hold the patch in place on the front panel.

I had earlier decided that I would use a butt joint and hammer weld this section in place, so before lighting the torch, I made sure my hammer and dolly were nicely to hand.

I put a couple of tack welds in position and hammered them against the dolly. This technique is fully described elsewhere in the book. Remember that hammering like this will cause little bits of hot debris to fall on your hand!

When I was sure that the patch was correctly located, I began to seam-weld all round. Weld a bit, hammer, weld a bit, hammer. That's the technique. The result is quite a tidy job. On the passenger side I had to let-in an extra piece of steel to replace some rust, it can be seen in the photograph, below the headlamp, and butt welded it to the main repair section.

The problem area was matching the outside edge of the patch to the wing. I used a half inch lip, formed at 90 degrees to the main panel. This lip had to be curved, so I cut out a series of 'V's in the lip to obtain the correct shape. This proved a little more difficult than I had anticipated, and I must admit I adopted the tactic of 'leave it for a day or two and it will look easier!' In fact this tactic often saves your temper if a job does not go too well. Pack up the tools for the day, or go and cut out some templates and sheet steel for another job. This

The secret of sectioning – clamp the two pieces of metal securely, and keep them about one sixteenth inch apart. Those Inter-grip clamps are just right for this sort of work.

takes your mind off the problem for a bit, and when you return to it at a later time, it often falls into place without too much effort. One day I cut out about a dozen patches, which made later jobs go that much quicker.

I was able to make the necessary adjustments, but as I said earlier if I had used a thinner gauge of steel the job would have been less difficult. The finished repair looks quite tidy. I'm not sure what you would pay for a new front panel these days, but if you reckon I spent 10 hours on the job and the costs were a piece of steel, some welding rods and some gas, then I reckon it was worth it. Instead of a sheet of steel, you could section in a piece cut from another front panel, perhaps one you got from a scrap yard. I'll tell you a bit more about that in a moment.

Sectioning can be used in many situations, from front wings, to doors, to front panels, rear panels, in fact anywhere where you can join new metal to old. Often with an old car it is your only choice – section in a part panel or scrap the car. There is the other alternative which is not covered in this book, which is make a panel from glass fibre. This can be done, but it *must not* be a structural panel – that is a load-bearing panel.

Scrapyards

One of the great benefits of sectioning is that you can often save a lot of money by using second-hand panels. The best source of second-hand panels is the scrap yard or breaker's yard, also known as vehicle dismantlers in this age of fancy job descriptions.

Scrap yards vary enormously, from little corners in a field to acres of partly dismantled cars. Prices vary a lot too, so it helps if you know how difficult it will be to find the item you are looking for. That way, you can judge if you are being ripped off.

Looks bad! Here I am piecing in part of the front panel. The square hole is for the sidelight, and I was able to salvage a mounting assembly for the lamp which goes behind the square.

I have used second-hand front panels, doors, wings, boot floor panels, bonnets, boot lids, B posts, and on one occasion I bought the complete rear quarter of a Volvo.

The best method of removing wings and front panels is the hammer and chisel. This method allows you to carry the minimum of tools, yet do a neat, tidy and quick removal job.

There are only a few things you need to remember when deciding where to cut. Know what you want, then make the mark a couple of inches away from the piece you want. This gives you a nice margin for cutting and allows you to tidy the item up back home. Normally the breaker's yard is not too worried where you cut, but make sure you discuss the job with the yard manager before you cut, otherwise you could be charged for damaging potentially valuable parts.

Remember to keep your chisel sharp and keep to the cutting line. A pencil is ideal for this sort of job. Occasionally, if you want a large section of car, the breaker might be persuaded to cut it off for you with the cutting torch. Be sure you both know where he is going to cut, otherwise you could waste the whole assembly.

I reckon I can remove the entire front end from a car in less than half an hour — just with hammer and chisel. I have done this several times, hacking off damaged Capri front ends in the hope of being able to salvage enough to complete repairs to mine. I remember paying about £10 for the whole front end! There are many bonuses doing this, as you also get all the clips, fasteners, brackets, rubber bushes and so on — the bits you don't get anywhere else. These alone can save pounds on a rebuild.

I got this 1963 Ford Capri front panel assembly for just £5 a few years ago. I was able to dismantle it and use some of the parts to repair my own front panel. Items like the 5-star bar and the chrome strip above it are hard to find now.

So have a fresh look at breaker's yards. If you need a chassis section, compare the price from the breaker's yard with the price of a new one, if you can find a new one. You can identify where one part ends and another begins from the manufacturers' Parts List which you should try to obtain for your car.

Jɪɢ-sᴀᴡɪɴɢ

There is another sectioning technique which I want to explain to you. It is like 'sectioning' only smaller! I call it 'jig-sawing' for want of a better title. It means that where you have a rusty panel with an involved shape, you piece-in small bits of steel just like the pieces in a jig-saw, until the required shape has been achieved. By 'small' I mean perhaps just an inch or so on each side.

The technique demands careful welding, but really spectacular results can be achieved. It takes time and a fair measure of confidence. The first time I saw this being put into practice I was astounded. The welder cut little pieces of steel about an inch wide and two inches long. He gave them a little of the required shape by tapping the edges with a hammer against the edge of a vice. Then he carefully placed the piece in the required position, held his breath, and got a tack weld on. After that, with the torch turned down really low, he ran beads of weld right round the patch. Afterwards, there was hardly any grinding to do to finish the job off. I reckon that the

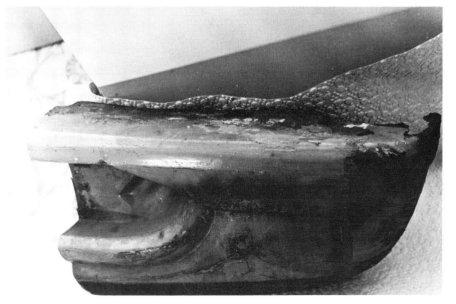

This is the right hand corner from the panel shown above. There is a little rust hole on the top edge, near the outer edge, but this can be repaired.

couple of hours the professional spent on my Capri front panel saved the car. It cost me some cash, but I learned a very valuable technique and it saved me searching for an expensive (if obtainable) new front panel.

You can use the same technique on your rebuild. Remember to keep all the edges of the steel clean and shiny, and to burn the torch at as low a pressure as you can manage with. Take your time, the results will be well worthwhile.

On one of my cars shown in this book, you will see that the rusty area round the headlamp has been repaired by sectioning in new steel. I could not afford a new wing at the time but wanted to try to tidy up the headlamp shell for the annual safety test. The front edge was formed around a new headlamp mounting ring. (It lies behind the headlamp and cannot be seen. It cost about £4). The repair consists of three pieces of steel and took a couple of hours to weld in place. The job could have been finished off properly with a skim of plastic filler. However, all it got was a quick spray over with undercoat. After a few months the rust broke through the thin layer of paint. However, the repair is photographed a full three years after it was done, so I reckon I got my money worth out of that repair. I'll be bringing that car into the workshop this Winter and I'll sort it out properly! The other way to tackle this type of repair is to use a new front wing repair section, which is already shaped to fit straight on.

Patching

The dictionary defines the word patch as a piece of material sewn or stuck to another to mend a hole. That definition will do quite well for us with one major reservation. The patch must NOT be on top of a rusty piece of steel.

To do this is absolutely pointless. The rusty steel will only spread its disease to the new steel and the whole problem will start all over again. So our patch must mend the hole, but must mend a clean, bright shiny hole. In other words you must prepare the area to be patched.

The types of patching jobs which you will be able to tackle are replacing pieces of chassis member, making good a rusted wing or doing some repair work to other panels such as the roof. Let's have a look at roof patching first.

Roof Patching

There is not much that can be done with a roof that has rusted. You could try cutting out the rusty part and welding in a new piece, but there are a number of problems associated with that approach. Let's have a look at the problems.

The first, and biggest problem is one of

A close up of a rusty front wing, showing a repair done three years before. It prolonged the life of the car long enough to prevent it being scrapped, and it is now being fully restored.

distortion. The roof is normally the largest, flattest area on the entire body and is not too well supported. Consequently, if you weld anywhere on the roof, you run a big risk of distorting it. There is another reason why it is difficult to weld a roof panel. Access to the steel. Just think for a moment about removing all the interior trim, especially the headlining!

Having initially put you off, let's have a look at what you *can* do. First, if the rust is localised, I would seriously consider a glass fibre job. It still means removing the headlining, but at least there is no risk of fire.

If you remove the headlining, you then have access to both sides of the rust. Grind out the rust, so that a hole is left with nice

clean shiny steel all round. Next, prepare some glass fibre material. You will need a bit of glass mat to bridge over the hole. This will go on the inside of the roof. Follow the instructions which come with the glass fibre kit. I don't want to dodge the issue, but each manufacturer of glass fibre has his own instructions, so follow those to the letter.

Once you have a patch on the inside of the roof, and it has hardened properly, mix up some plastic filler which is then applied to the outside of the roof. This needs to be rubbed down well, to achieve a nice blend in with the steel roof. Don't lean too hard, or you will distort the roof panel with your weight.

If you decide to weld the roof panel, (this is a decision YOU must make, as I cannot advise on individual jobs) follow these guidelines.

The sort of job I want to describe is a small localised rust spot on the roof. I have a small spot like this on my Capri, and it began when the previous owner stored tins of paint on top of the roof, in a leaky garage. Now I have to repair one round spot of serious rust — about an inch or so in diameter.

First, remove all headlining and other trim. Make sure there is no wiring run along the inside of the roof gutter. Remove all fire hazards.

Drill out the rust spot with the electric drill. This will help to minimise distortion, as you will not have to press too hard to drill through the rust. Next, fit a tapered grinding stone in the drill, and grind out the rust spot until you have shiny, sound metal all round. Ensure that all the rust is gone.

Now take a small piece of scrap steel, and hold it on the underside of the roof, so that it covers the hole. (You might need some help with this, depending on the location of the spot). Draw on the steel, through the hole in the roof, so that you have a small, circular patch marked out.

The patch needs to be about one sixteenth of an inch smaller all round, than the hole. I have already described how to attach a small piece of welding rod to a patch like this. Now I'll tell you another way.

When you finish marking out the patch, add a little mark on either side of the patch, so that you leave a little triangular finger of steel. When you cut out the patch, bend this little triangle — mind your fingers — so that the steel patch sits into the hole in the roof, and is supported by the triangles. With a little bit of adjustment, you can get the patch to sit exactly where you want it.

Now comes the tricky bit — the welding. Clean all round the hole on the outside of the roof. You need all the paint off for about half an inch round the hole. This will allow you a quicker, cleaner weld.

When the paint is off, put a few tack welds, opposite the supporting triangles. Very carefully, melt the small triangular supports into the roof panel. Don't worry if you leave a little lump, you will need to finish off with the grinder anyway.

You can weld a little, then gently hammer the weld with hammer and dolly. Alternatively, if you can control the flame well enough, just move gently round the patch with a low flame and melt a little filler rod into the join. Take your time.

When the welding is complete, tap the area with a hammer and dolly. The dolly

This headlamp panel for the Ford Classic and Capri is available from the Consul Capri Owners Club. You can see how it has been fabricated from several pieces.

should be a close match to the contours of the roof. When you are satisfied with the repair, grind it smooth, and apply a skim of filler as described in the Chapter, Paint and Protect.

A final word of warning when welding. If anything does catch fire, it will drop from the roof and ignite anything underneath. Don't get caught. If you are in any doubt about welding, remove everything from the car. I have an asbestos blanket which I keep wet, and spread it over areas likely to be troublesome. Even so, I take special care when tackling this sort of job, because it is so easy to encounter a problem you did not anticipate.

I have seen two cars on fire. One belonged to a friend of mine who was using my welding equipment. He was doing a small welding job on the floor of his 1600E, but one of the seats caught fire, and before we knew what had happened the inside of the car was badly damaged.

The other experience was my fuel-injected Volvo. I can't prove it, but it seems a

It pays to get hold of a workshop manual as soon as possible. The manufacturers Parts List is also handy for showing how things are assembled.

Wish I had a Wheeling machine. These machines are ideal for forming small patches and repair sections. They need a lot of skill to get the best results from them.

petrol pipe failed, and the pump sprayed petrol all over the engine. The entire front of the car was destroyed. That was my one and only fuel-injected car. Never again!

Now, there is a point to all this. That is, you find it difficult to appreciate how quickly a fire can spread. In the time it takes to read this little, short, paragraph, your car has now caught fire, and the trim and roof lining are ablaze.

It is staggering how quickly a fire can spread. I had to watch the Volvo burn while the Fire Brigade arrived. In about five minutes the front of the car was gutted. Don't take any chances when welding, it just is not worth it.

Roof Pillar Patching

Basically, there is little to say under this heading. If you have rust or damage, then the procedure is the same as for all other jobs:

Assess the damage, mark out the area to be repaired, cut a template if necessary, remove the damaged steel, weld in the new and finish with plastic filler or lead.

Occasionally, you will be able to obtain a new 'second-hand' part for the one damaged on your car. Scrapyards are a great source of spares, but all too many people think of them as sources of mechanical parts. If the body part or chassis part is sound and rust free, then it can be transplanted to your car and prolong its life.

Chassis Patching

A typical job is at the front of the main chassis member, where the bumper brackets bolt through the chassis. Over the years this area usually deteriorates and requires attention.

The first thing to do is remove the bumper bar bolts. This is often quite tricky if they have rusted into place, but a heavy dose of penetrating oil will help, especially if it is allowed to soak in for 24 hours. If the bolts won't shift after that time, or you are in a hurry, get out the gas welding torch. Have

"HAGLEY HALL, HERE WE COME!"

JULY 1987

The front cover of the July 1987 Cortina MKI Owners Club. Joining the club is the first thing you should do after buying your MKI.

Patching the inner sill. New steel has been tack welded in place and here a seam weld is being run. On this repair I tried joggling the lower edge of the repair panel to get a more realistic finish. You can just see the ridge along the lower edge.

the correct size spanners or sockets ready and then apply a gentle heat to the nut. Get it nice and hot (just approaching red heat is best) then get the spanners on quickly. Nine times out of ten the nut will move, but it may be accompanied by a wailing and screeching sound! If you are quick with the spanners, you may be able to get each nut undone with just one application of heat. If not, repeat the process, but remember that the longer the spanner is on a red-hot nut, the hotter the spanner will get. Fingers burn easily!

Once the nuts are off, tap the bolts out gently with a hammer. Normally you should replace bolts which have been treated (or rather mis-treated) this way, but for items like bumper bolts which have no stresses you can get away with cleaning them up and using them again. However if you are in any doubt about their condition, replace them.

Now you can inspect the rusty area. It will probably be a bit more extensive than you thought. Scrape off any remaining underseal with a wire brush or scraper, then tap all round the area with a screwdriver or small hammer. Once you have found how extensive the rust is, you can start to plan the replacement patch.

Cut out the damaged area with the hammer and chisel. You could use an oxygen-rich flame in the welding torch, but ensure that you do not distort any sound metal that you want to weld to.

Once the chassis box section is opened up – for you are almost always repairing the flat panel which makes up the fourth side of a top-hat section – clean out any remaining rust and debris. If the chassis section has captive bolts, for example on the anti-roll bar mountings, then this is a good time to add some penetrating oil to these bolts and work them loose and tight a couple of times. This will ensure that the next time you need to remove them, they will come out cleanly. If they don't come out cleanly, you would have to open up the chassis section to repair them, which is the position you are in now. Prevention is better than cure.

Now get your template kit, as described in the first Chapter. You need some brown paper, a pair of scissors, a pencil and some cardboard. Using the brown paper, make a template for the required patch. Have a look back at the first Chapter if you've forgotten what to do.

For a patch like this I like to use the technique where the patch is made one sixteenth of an inch smaller, all round, than the hole. The reason for this is simple. The little gap allows room for expansion, and saves distorting the patch as it is welded in place. The result is a neater job.

You might be thinking, okay, how do I hold this type of patch in place before I

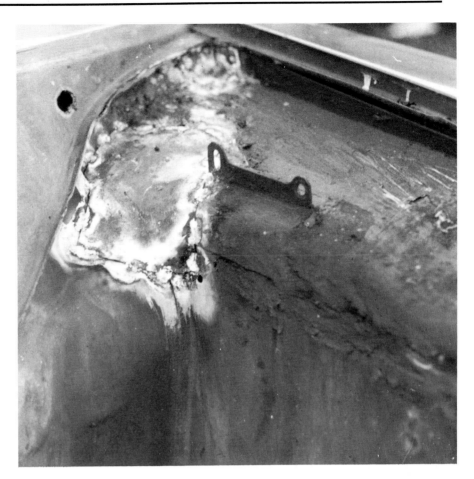

A patch at the corner of the front bulkhead and the inner wing. The bracket with the two holes is for the hood or bonnet hinge. (Photo by Roger Raisey.)

weld. There are a couple of answers to that, such as Mole clamps, or C clamps. There is another simple little technique which you may like to remember. It can save many an awkward situation.

When you have the patch cut exactly to the required shape, get a short length of welding rod, and weld the end of the rod onto the middle of the patch, so that the welding rod is at right angles to the surface of the patch. Then bend the welding rod to suit the situation and use the welding rod to position the patch. After a few tack welds are in place, you can 'waggle' the welding rod to break it free of the patch. When you come to finish off the job there

I welded this strengthening patch on the underside of my modified outrigger. The square steel washer serves to locate the Ford jack. (You are looking up at the outrigger from underneath.)

will be a tiny little lump of weld in the middle of the patch which can be easily removed with a grinder or a file.

PATCHING TOP HAT

This is one of the most common patching jobs you will encounter during a restoration. It is also one of those jobs which can be badly done with the same effort as doing it properly. On almost every rusty old car I have bought, there has been a patch welded (and I use this word in its broadest sense) on top of a rusty chassis section. The welding usually looks like it has been thrown on from a distance using a technique which my welding instructor once aptly described as 'chicken-shit welding.' I always associate this type of repair with a mechanic who has never mastered the welding torch. It is one of the reasons my Capri rebuild is taking so long. Almost everything underneath which was 'repaired' has had to be repaired again. Follow this advice given here and do it right.

In another Chapter I showed you how to fabricate new sides and bottom for a rusty chassis section. In this bit I will show you the correct way to patch one side of a 'Top Hat' chassis section. For the sake of an example, let's say that the bottom section in a piece of chassis has rusted and you have to repair it. You'll need some steel, welding equipment and a small grinding stone mounted in an electric drill.

Remove any paint and underseal covering the rusty area. When this is done, prod the steel with a screwdriver or sharp spike. You need to know the full extent of the damage before you plan the repair. When you know exactly the extent of the damage, go on to the next step.

If the bottom of the chassis section is flat, then you will probably not need to make a template. Just hold the new steel against the bottom of the chassis and scribe round the area you need for the patch. Remember that the patch marked out will be larger than what you actually need, because you are marking round the *outside* of the Top Hat. If you feel you need a template, please make one.

When the patch is marked out or a template made, get the electric drill and grind out the damaged area. This should be quite easy to do with a grinding stone. I find that the tapered ones give the best results. When the rust is ground away, and you have shiny new steel on all sides, smooth off the area by grinding the edges of the chassis. You don't want any sharp edges to cut yourself on.

Offer up the patch again. This time you may have to trim it to fit. You will get a neater job if you leave that one sixteenth inch gap between patch and chassis, but you may find it easier to overlap the patch

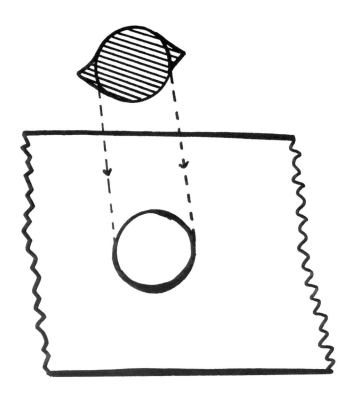

If you need to cut out a small patch, leave two little lips — one on each side — to locate the patch in the hole. The lips can be welded in later.

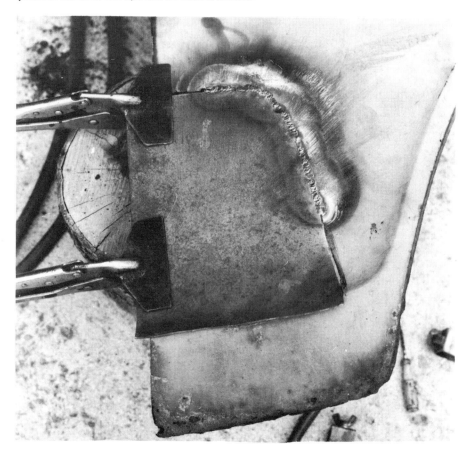

Patching a front wing. Here the patch is being seam welded. The full repair of this wing is illustrated elsewhere in the book.

The main chassis being repaired. This view is of the main chassis, just behind the MacPherson strut tower. The rusty section has been removed and the spot welds ground flat. A small localised repair is needed on the bottom of the chassis member, and this will be done after the repair patch is welded in place.

This view shows the repair patch held in place by clamps while I check for fit. I decided to use this repair patch although it did not cover the area of rust. For most cars this patch will be ideal. Mine had extra rust above the main chassis member, on the inner wing which was repaired with another little patch.

onto good steel. Either way, decide which course of action you want to follow and stick to it.

When the patch is ready, fix it in position by whatever method you find the best. I would use the screw jack, as described elsewhere in the book. For this job I would put a small piece of wood between the jack and the patch. This allows better access to the patch with the welding equipment.

Check the adjacent areas of the car before welding. Don't leave anything inflammable near the welding area. Once the patch is located, get a couple of tack welds on. When this is done, you can remove the jack. Then its just a matter of seam welding the patch in place.

Two more tips. First, if you choose to cut the patch bigger than the hole, you can simply melt the excess edge of the patch into the side of the chassis section. When I say the patch is bigger I mean perhaps one sixteenth of an inch bigger. Any larger than that and you are not doing the job properly. This melting in will save using filler rod, and can be an easier job if you are lying underneath the car. I favour this method.

Secondly, if you choose to cut the patch smaller than the hole, you will have to leave a couple of triangular supports as described under roof repairs. These will allow the patch to be correctly located, flush with the existing steel.

Overlap Patching

Overlap patching can occur in many cases, for example when joining a new chassis leg to the remains of the old one. Generally, you would overlap the new over the old, but you may wish to overlap the old over

The top of the MacPherson strut is a common place for rust. Patches are available, but there is no point welding one on top of rust. You will only have more, and bigger, problems in a year or so. (Photo by Roger Raisey.)

the new. Either way will be acceptable, as long as a neat job is done and it keeps water out of the join.

One of the problems with overlap joins is that when you apply heat to one piece of steel, the other tends to buckle slightly and move away from the heat source. This tendency can be discouraged by careful clamping, but there are some basic facts which need to be remembered.

If you apply heat, such as a welding flame, to a painted surface, the surface will start to heat up. But because there is a layer of paint in the way, the steel will not heat up as quickly as a shiny, unpainted piece of steel. So you need to apply more heat until the paint begins to burn off. By this time the steel has absorbed more heat than was necessary and has probably buckled.

The answer is simple, remove all paint and underseal before welding. Clean shiny metal welds much easier than painted metal.

Having got that little problem out of the way, what else can you do to make a good overlap join? There are several things you can do. First you can apply a clamp, such as a C clamp to the two parts to be joined. However, if you are joining Top Hat to Top Hat, such as the chassis leg described above, your clamp would need to open up to take both sides of the section. This might work, but if you tighten up the clamp too tightly, you might crush the sides of the section.

Another way to hold an overlap is to drill

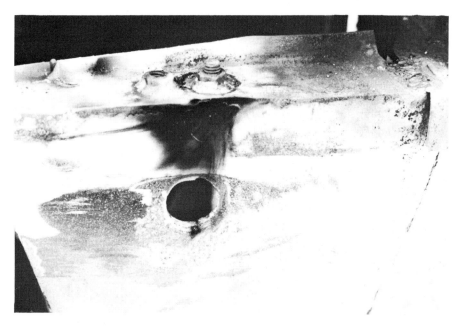

This is the lower, front corner panel on the Ford Capri. I have brazed the nut in place, holding it by tightening the bolt. The captive bolts hold a bumper bar mounting.

through both thicknesses of steel and clamp them together with a pop-rivet. This works well but takes extra time and can be a bit of a fiddle.

You could drill a hole and use a couple of Wedgelock-type fasteners for this job. This is probably a better bet than pop rivets.

Another way is to open out the sides of the section going 'inside' so that a really tight fit is achieved. This can often be the best answer to the problem.

So, to recap, clean off both surfaces to allow quicker, cleaner welding. This will cut down distortion and make for a neater job.

Double Overlap Patching

I have used this method a number of times, including a conversion job when I made my Volvo pickup. I had to cut through the roof panel, right from one side of the car to the other. Then I had to cut again just in front of the rear windscreen surround. The rear windscreen surround was then moved forward to meet the new end of the roof panel. I then had to join the two parts.

After a bit of thought I decided to use a method which I have called double overlap for want of a better description. Having two pieces of steel (the two bits of roof) which had to end up at the same level, I had a few choices. I could butt them together and weld, I could joggle one edge and weld, or I could lay one edge over the other, weld and finish of smooth with filler. I decided against all of these.

I instead cut a narrow strip of steel, about six inches wide and as long as the distance from one side of the roof to the other. I then located this panel under the two pieces of roof. When the welds were run, it left a wide, shallow groove which could be filled with plastic filler.

This method might not have suited everyone, but I figured that the join was right above where I would be sitting and I didn't want it to leak on my head. It meant two welding runs instead of one, but did offer a re-inforcing plate underneath which helped to prevent the roof panels distorting. It worked for me!

You can apply similar principles to joining two bits of chassis member. Instead of overlapping them, you can add an extra piece which lies over (or under, if you can arrange it) both parts. Weld it in place and smooth off with the grinder.

I hope I have given you some ideas for patching and sectioning. Don't be put off if you don't get good results first time. If in doubt about the technique, try it out on some scrap first. In the next Chapter I want to show you how to apply some of these techniques to Outer Panels — the bits that are seen, and the panels by which your metalwork is judged!

To show what is available, I have included this advert from Classic Components who have a lot of MKI Cortina repair panels available. Remember that prices may vary from those shown.

The engine compartment of a 1937 Chevrolet Coach. Although much of the metalwork looks bad, you can almost feel the thickness of the steel from the photograph. Most of this could be restored. (Photo by Terry Hill.)

I found this Morris Minor wing dumped in a ditch. The rust line up the wing is typical of the model. If this was the only wing available, could you repair it by welding in some new metal? Luckily, new wings are available at reasonable cost.

This is the front wing of a very rare 1954 Studebaker Commander. This rust looks bad, and would need a big repair section to restore it. What would you do? (Photo by Terry Hill.)

Below, the entire left hand side of this car has been sectioned and patched from small bits of steel. Other photos in this book show the work being done.

Right, this sketch shows the method of using a small patch piece as a double overlap join. This technique is useful in many cases and you should remember it when planning particular jobs. If the situation allows the patch can go on the 'inside' and the two pieces being joined are levelled with plastic filler.

Below, another view of a front panel being rebuilt. Although it looks untidy and ugly, this is the half finished job, so don't judge too harshly. The job is finished off neat and tidy now, and the car takes me to work every day.

TO JOIN:

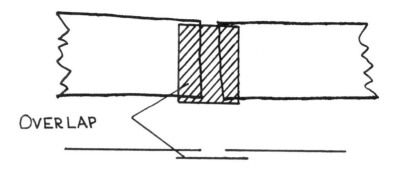

OVERLAP

SIDE VIEW

TO PATCH:

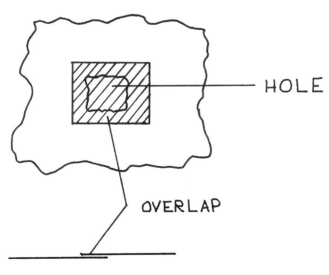

HOLE

OVERLAP

SIDE VIEW

The front wing or fender of this 1955 Pontiac looks a prime candidate for some patching work.

Left, the sketch shows a repair patch overlapping the hole. This is a common repair method but needs extra work to disguise the join. You could, of course, weld the patch 'behind' the hole and finish the surface with plastic filler. Sometimes this is not possible due to access problems.

Outer Panels

The ugly patches round the headlamp spoil the looks of this car. The repair took just a few hours and gave the car another three years of life. It is now undergoing a full restoration.

In this Chapter I want to look at the outer panels on the car such as wings, front and rear valances etc. There are many ways to save money on a restoration and you can often repair a wing or door with a little time and effort after someone else has thrown it away. Remember what we said about 'shape' in Chapter One. Its going to play a big part in this Chapter too.

Lets start with front wings. Basically there are two types — the kind that bolt on such as on the British Morris Minor, Ford Capri and Classic, and the Swedish Volvo 140, and the kind that are welded on such as the Mini, Cortina etc. Although there are two methods of fixing, you still have the same problems, such as rust or accident damage. The only helpful thing about bolt-on wings is that you can usually remove them cleanly without resorting to the hammer and chisel, necessary for the welded on kind.

It is likely that certain areas of the wing will suffer from rust more than others. These areas are usually around the head-lamps, along the edge where they attach to the inner wing, and at the bottom where the lower rear part of the wing meets the front of the sill. I think the photographs will emphasise what you might already know!

If your wing is from a very rare car, you may have no choice but to repair it. Find out what is available. Can you get a new wing? Is it too expensive? Okay, can you get repair patches from your auto dealer? No, again? Don't worry. We can make patches which will be hard to spot once you have finished.

One of the commonest rust areas is around the headlamps. This area collects all the mud and dirt thrown up from the front wheels and keeps a nice damp lump of the stuff all round the headlamp bowl. No wonder it rusts.

Lets say you have not been able to find a new wing, but you have found a replacement panel. The one in the photographs cost about £10. You will also need a new bowl to set the headlamp in, and I have used a plastic bowl which will never rust out. It costs about £5 but as far as I know, you can only get them for seven-inch head-lamps.

Once you have the parts to hand, mark off the area on the wing you want to cut. *STOP right now!* I have made a mistake here which I want you to think about.

In the last paragraph I said mark off the area to cut *after you had bought the new parts.* You should have done that bit first. Please don't think I am being silly in the way I pointed this out. I still do it so many times too!

When you measure out how much rust you have to replace, you will have to ask the makers of the replacement panel what size it is. For example, if you need to cut three inches from the front of your wing, call the makers and ask if their panel extends three or more inches from the front of the wing. If it does you are okay. If it doesn't then you may be able to extend it with some extra steel.

When you are sure the replacement will fit, mark off the area to cut with a pencil. If your new panel is three inches long, you need to make a mark about three and one sixteenth from the front. This allows the two panels to butt-together with one sixteenth inch between for the weld. Check your measurements once again, then cut the rusty part of the old wing off. I use tin snips for this sort of job, but you may want to use a hacksaw or another kind of panel cutter. Any method is all right as long as you don't distort the shape in the wing.

When the old part is off, clean up the cut with a file. This prevents slivers of steel causing injuries later on.

Offer up the new panel to check the fit. You may find that two sides are a good fit, but you need to take a little more off either the old wing or the new panel. Make this decision carefully, for once you cut it off it is difficult to put back.

When you get a good fit, join the two panels with clamps, welding clamps or whatever other sorts of fixings you have. When its fixed, stand back and look carefully.

NOW is the time to get it right. Not when you have started to weld. Are the two panels in a straight line? What I mean is, if you lay a straight edge along what should be straight do you have a hollow or a lump? Neither is good, but you can at least fill in a hollow with filler. Remember, you can get reference measurements from the same panel on the other side of your car.

Having got the two parts together and lined up to your satisfaction, (remember you might have to live with it for a long time if you keep the car), get the welding torch ready.

The secret of this sort of job is to clean both edges of the steel with a grinder or wire brush. Do NOT rely on the heat of the torch burning off dirt and paint. This is a shoddy way to tackle the job and you will get a shoddy finish. Get both parts nice and shiny, then select a small nozzle for your torch. For a job like this, I would use a number 1 nozzle on my BOC Sapphire torch. I also recommend one sixteenth inch welding rods. These encourage a neat finish.

Rear Valances

Rear valances or rear skirts collect all the mud, dirt and debris thrown up from the road. In Britain and North America where a lot of salt is used in the Winter, the rear valance can disintegrate in next to no time. Depending on the condition, you can repair or replace. Either way, you are going to have to remove the rear bumper which often bolts through the rear valance into

I have started to cut off the front part of the wing, which is to have a new front section welded in. You can see the remains of the previous glass fibre 'repair'.

The new repair section clamped in position. Make sure everything is spot-on before welding. (The patch is available from Classic Components.)

the chassis leg. You may have to use lots of penetrating oil to get the bolts out. If you are not too close to the petrol tank, get the welding torch lit and heat the captive nuts on the chassis leg. Then get a socket wrench on the nuts and remove them. Heat works most times. The nuts may squeal as they come off, but you will save yourself time later if you get the nuts out clean.

Repairing Rear Valances

As with all the other body jobs, the secret is to assess the extent of the damage before you do anything else. Scrape off paint if you have to, and don't be afraid to prod with a spike or screwdriver. Only when you have mapped out the whole rusty area can you begin to plan the repair.

For instance, if you have a basically sound valance, with a lot of rust on one corner (as in the photograph) you can repair it in two or three pieces. Don't be afraid of tackling a corner repair. With a little skill and the help of some cardboard templates you can produce a really smart corner without any special tools.

If you are tackling a corner replacement, make sure you make your cardboard patterns BEFORE you cut steel. Even the cutting action of a sharp pair of snips can distort rusty steel. And you don't want to lose the shape. Cut away the rotted steel but DON'T THROW IT AWAY. Why

The patch welded in position, and some additional work started on the front panel. Make sure that headlamp ring is correctly located before welding!

junk a small bit of steel till the job is complete? If you make a mistake, you still have the original shape to go back to. Refer to the first Chapter for advice about shaping a curved surface.

The rear valance on this Volvo had been hacked away to allow room for a tow-bar. A new 'middle valance' section was made up and welded in. I had forgotten that I'd done this repair until I found this photo!

Forming a Corner

This skill involves making a compound curve. I usually try to explain what that is by describing a football. From any point on the surface of the football, the ball curves in all directions.

Now think of a steel wheel rim, like on a Western covered wagon. From a point on the surface of the rim, the steel curves away in only two directions. Say it curves to left and right when you look at it. If you now look ahead, the steel is almost flat. Across any piece of the rim, the steel is almost flat. But in the other direction it curves. Got the idea? Now back to the football.

Suppose you need to make a corner for the front of your wing or front panel. You decide that it is a compound curve. How do you make this? You need your old friend the template kit again.

You will need to make up two (possibly even three templates) for this job. The trick is to get them as near as possible to the correct shape, then join them by welding.

Mentally split the curved panel into two. Cut out some brown paper and make the first template, usually the bigger of the two pieces. Get this exactly right. You will probably have to cut out a 'V' in the paper to get the shape right. The more 'V's, the more welding you have to do. Make sure the 'V's are cut out properly, for they control how accurate the finished job will be. Get the two templates exactly right. When you weld the two together you will

This panel is actually a sill for a Vauxhall Viva HC. I'm presently adapting it to make a new valance for my MKI Cortina. It cost just £5.

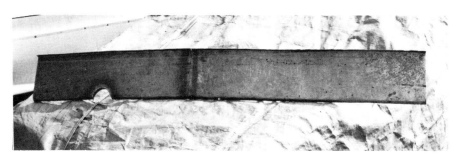

I made this valance up a long time ago, but was never happy with it, because it lacks style. You can see where it was made in two pieces. It might help you to make one for your car.

You can just see the welding runs on this repaired corner. Look to the left and right of the bumper-bar bolt.

have part of a sphere. This is your corner.

I made a steel skirt with curved corners for one of my cars. I needed two templates in paper, followed by two pieces of steel. It is not difficult to do.

Replacing Rear Valances

If you are lucky enough to have a replacement valance for your collector car you have saved yourself some time, but spent a little more money. When you get the valance back home, offer it up to the original to make sure it is the correct part. You are going to feel a bit sick if you cut the old one off then find the new one doesn't fit!

I'll assume that you have removed all the bumper-bar and fittings and anything else which might be in the way, such as a number plate lamp assembly. These are sometimes held onto the valance by self-tapping screws.

When you are sure it will fit (and there is no harm in taking measurements to be sure) start to remove the old valance.

Very often there is a lip where the rear panel of the car meets the valance. This lip might face in towards the car, or outwards where it becomes a styling feature. If there is a lip, get your chisel in between the two pieces of steel and break the spot welds. Do this as neatly as possible, because the area is one which will be seen on the finished car.

Having released all along the top of the valance, you now have to detach it from the rear quarter panels, in other words down the outside edges of the valance. This again is a chisel job, but it needs a lot of care if you are not to damage the quarter panel.

Once the valance is off, clean up all the attaching points with a wire brush, followed by a grinder if necessary. I like to get any spot welds ground down flat, as they can cause lumps between the rear panel and the valance if they are not removed.

Now try the new valance for fit. You might need help for this, as its difficult to hold both ends at the same time. You might be able to use some Mole clamps to hold one end while you locate the other end. Another help is to put the bolts for the bumper-bar brackets back. With a couple of big flat washers they will help to accurately locate the valance. Try to get a really good fit, sincethis is the sort of panel which can spoil the looks of a car if you leave a tatty, unfinished or badly fitted job.

Once you are satisfied with the fit, clamp the valance in its final position and put some tack welds in place. For this sort of job I would want two or three on the long edge of the valance and one or two along each outer edge. That way it is securely held.

Because it is not a structural member of the car, (that is it takes no load and provides little strength, being mostly decorative), it does not have to be seam welded. I leave this decision to you. I would weld an inch or so, then leave a couple of inches free. Make sure you hammer the two unwelded edges together though, to prevent water seaping in between. Once you have painted it properly it should keep water out anyway.

I would weld all of the outer edges where they join to other panels. This is just a personal choice, but I feel it makes a stronger corner, which would be useful if you encounter any parking damage!

Glass Fibre Parts

I must be honest right at the start of this section. I have had very little experience of glass fibre panels. All of it has been bad.

I read reports in all the car club magazines about panels which would not fit and vowed I would never have glass panels on any of my cars. I resisted for years until I saw the chance to cut weeks off a restoration and get a car on the road before the Winter set in. I ordered two front wings from what I thought was one of the best manufacturers around. They cost a little bit more than the rest, and after a discussion on the phone with the makers, I ordered.

When they arrived they looked good. No blemishes or other problems. As soon as I offered them up to the car I found they would not fit. Where there should have been a lip of one and a half inches to mount onto the body, there was only one inch. That meant when I drilled the mounting holes, they broke through the lip edge.

Whatever I did the wings would not fit. I tried all sorts of things and then made the fatal mistake of cutting steel off the car to try to get the glass wings to fit. I spent more than two days working on a wing, trying to get it to fit. If the front fitted neatly, the rear fouled the door. In the end I consigned them to the shed, and there they remain, £50 of hard-earned lesson.

The author's Volvo pick-up, built to transport motorcycles. It did the job well but I spent too long on the conversion to make it worthwhile.

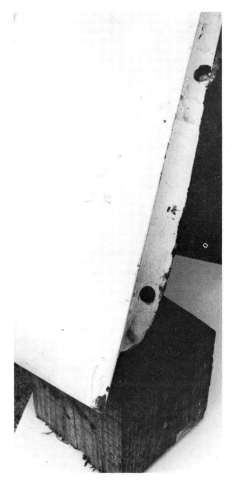

The dreaded glass fibre wing. This mounting flange is about three quarters of an inch wider on the correct steel wing.

I also bought a rear valance for the same car. It cost around £9 and seemed to fit okay. Remember you have to drill all the holes yourself on a glass panel. I drilled my holes (they were okay) but I then decided I could make my own valance — including a compound curve — in steel. I went out and made the valance and was delighted with the result. The glass valance lies in the shed too.

Now, I have spoken to people who have bought glass panels and they say they fit perfectly. So let me leave the subject like this. They are much cheaper than steel. They are available when steel is often not available. Don't get caught. Try before you buy. If they don't fit when you try one — forget it. It really is not worth the hassle. I could have repaired two steel wings in half the time it took me wrestling with the glass wings. As it is I have reverted to two patched steel wings, one of which is photographed for you to see. Anyway, by the time you finish reading Panel Craft you will be able to tackle the repair of steel wings!

If you decide to try your luck with glass fibre, here are a few tips gleaned from all the best books! Use large pop-rivets to secure panels. Alternatively, if the car had bolt-on wings, you can use the original bolts to hold the glass wings. Make sure you use large flat washers to spread the load, otherwise the glass may crack under compression.

Making Pick-ups

A number of people, including myself, like the idea of building a pick-up from a saloon car or estate car. The estate car idea is often the better choice, as the design of the rear tailgate often lends itself to being modified.

I bought a Volvo saloon (a 144 model) for £50 after it had suffered rear end damage after a close encounter with a Glasgow bus. At the time I was riding trials motorcycles, so I thought a pick-up would be nice to carry the bikes on. You can see the result in the photographs, taken during the re-build.

Basically, I cut out the roof between the rear windscreen and the B post then took the rear windscreen panel and moved it forward until it met up with the B post. I welded it into position. Using the boot lid as material I made up a new bulkhead, below the rear windscreen panel. I seam welded the rear doors shut to increase the strength of the shell, and made up a 'sill' to go along the tops of the rear doors and rear quarter panels. A few lengths of angle iron formed a bike rack on the rear of the bulkhead.

The weld across the entire width of the car, along the rear windscreen panel was important — not only for strength, but to keep out the weather. I can honestly say that it never leaked during the two years I had it.

You can make a tailgate from the original tailgate panel if you have cut down an estate car, or carefully cut out the middle section of the rear panel — the panel which runs between the rear lamps. A couple of hinges and some wiring for the number plate lamp and that's another job done.

I attached a couple of cheap handles on the sides to use when lashing-down the motor bikes. There was one legal requirement which I fell foul of in the first M.O.T Test (Safety Test). The petrol tank must be protected and shielded, so I had to fit a cover panel over the entire petrol tank.

This was not a bad thing, as it helped provide a stronger, straighter floor in the pick-up bed. The hump over the rear axle can be a nuisance though, depending on the sort of load you want to carry. My pick-up was a two-seater, but I later helped a friend build a four-seater from a Volvo estate.

I have also seen pick-ups made from a Ford Classic (see photograph), a couple of Triumph 2000s, and a Mazda saloon. The Austin Marina had a pick-up version available, but someone built one from a saloon as well! The last photograph in the book (in 'Tailpiece') shows the only view we got of a Cortina MKI pick-up/convertible. If the owner gets in touch, we can take some nicer photographs for the next edition of Panel Craft!

If you want to build a pick-up, consider the strength of the bodyshell, and also if you have the skill to do the job. You may have to weld in strengthening pieces to support the chassis, as the large roof area you are removing provides a lot of strength to the shell. The conversion has to be done 'neat and tidy', otherwise it will attract the attention of the Traffic Police every time you drive it.

This Ford Classic pick-up appeared at Hagley Hall in 1986. It provides the owner with distinctive transportation. Conversions like this need to be well thought-out before you reach for the tools!

TRAILERS

Many people have discovered the idea of cutting a van in half and making it into a covered trailer. The photograph shows a Cortina Estate modified this way. I have not seen underneath this particular conversion, but the problem areas will be attaching the tow-bar frame to the existing chassis. This has to be done absolutely right, otherwise you will have a heavily-loaded trailer try to overtake you on the road, as the coupling frame breaks off.

What are you going to do about brakes? Find out what the latest legislation is about trailer brakes, then plan how to comply.

If you are in any doubt about doing this sort of conversion, seek help from the Owner's Club. They will know of someone who has already done it.

Also, there is a very useful book called 'The Trailer Manual' which is published in the UK by Mechanical Services (Trailer Engineers) Ltd, PO Box 20, Bolton, BL1 2RP.

I have seen trailers made this way from Minis, Cortinas and Morris 1000 Travellers.

The front corner of the Ford Capri has been made from several sections. The headlamp panel and some other panels for this corner are available from the Consul Capri Owner's Club.

Chopping Roofs

This has been a popular pastime in America for a number of years, where I believe the process is known as a 'Top Chop.' Basically, you cut through the roof-supporting pillars, cut a bit out of them and then weld the roof back on. It sounds easy when you say it, but I tried it once on a Cortina and it really is difficult to do.

The problem can be highlighted by thinking of 'shape' yet again. The roof pillars normally taper towards the top, that is they are broad at the bottom and slim at the top. If you cut a bit out of the middle, the two remaining pieces will not fit together. (Draw it out on paper, then cut out the paper shape. You will soon see the problem).

Some of you might think, 'Ah, yes but if I cut a bit from the bottom, or a bit from the top, I can re-weld the pillar to the roof or rear quarter panel.' Well, you are half right! The additional problem is that the roof pillars are much wider at the bottom than at the top. That is, they taper towards the top. This means additional work.

If you want to do this sort of thing, which is more a 'hot rodding' procedure than a 'restoring' procedure — be very careful before you start. It will be more difficult, and take much longer than you expect. Once you finish the roof, what are you going to do about cutting down the doors, and the windscreen, and the rear screen and? and? You have to plan this sort of job ultra-carefully. I would not recommend it.

Louvres

Louvres can make a very nice addition to a modified car, and would be essential if you were fabricating an engine cover panel for an old sports car. They used to be difficult to make, but a hardwood former is now available which makes them quite easy to fabricate. The photographs show what can be done in the home workshop. The manufacturer's address is given at the end of the book.

Repairing a Wing

Lets have a close look at a repair job on a wing. I chose a wing to repair and removed it from a car in a breaker's yard. The yard manager took £15 for it, which I thought was a bit too much, but anyway it can be repaired and brought back to 'as new' condition for about £10.

In the yard I chiselled the wing off, taking care to leave plenty of metal next to the joining flanges. This ensures that when I came to tidy up all the edges, I am not left with extra work making up a new mounting flange.

I like to get the feel of a wing before I start serious repairs. I like to handle it, clean all the paint and underseal from underneath,

Well, this is different! Another Hagley Hall photograph, this time a Cortina estate trailer with its own Public Address system.

and generally find out how strong the wing is. Sometimes a wing will feel very different from another one from the same make and model. I don't know if the manufacturers ever made 'heavy' and 'light' wings, but I have noticed a big variation in the weight of wings.

Along the top edge of the wing, where I removed it from the car, is a lot of scrap metal still attached to the wing. This has to come off. There are several ways to do this, but I use a heavy pair of pliers followed by the angle grinder.

I use the pliers to get hold of a piece of scrap and wind the scrap round the pliers as though I were opening a sardine tin. You should find that with a bit of a twisting effort the spot welds will give way.

That darned glass fibre wing again! I never did get it to fit, despite repeated attempts.

You should end up with all the scrap wrapped round the pliers and a nice clean edge. However, things never work out that way and you will probably find that you have to wind off a bit at a time. It should only take about 10 minutes to clean up this edge. Before straightening all the edges and flanges, I want to clean up some of the spot welds broken during dismantling. I use an angle grinder for this, but if you don't have this tool available you can do just as good a job using an electric drill with a grinding stone attachment. *WEAR GOGGLES*.

When the top edge is clean and tidy, dress the edge with hammer and dolly. The first stage of the wing restoration has been completed.

For this exercise, I am going to straighten up the flange on the wing where it meets the mounting flange in front of the car door. Since I chiselled this off to break the spot welds, it needs grinding, dressing and straightening. For the grinding use an angle grinder or grinding stone as described above. Then I use the edge setter and a hammer and dolly.

First, I move along the flange with the edge setter, straightening as best I can. There will still be lumps where spot welds were broken, but you can ignore these for the moment. The reason for not grinding

What NOT to do. The hole in the front of this Capri wing should have been trimmed properly, before cutting out a patch. In the right hand photo you can see the difficult task facing the welder. Far better to spend ten minutes producing a 'square' patch with a one sixteenth inch gap ALL ROUND.

this area first is that it tends to be a bit weaker and will be more uneven after chiselling. So, before I can grind I must straighten. (I might have to straighten a second time after I grind though. Be prepared to do this).

Having straightened the flange as best you can, get the hammer and dolly and finish off any obstinate sections of steel which might not want to be straightened.

Now get the grinder and clean off all the broken spot welds. Check that all is nice and tidy, and you can go on to the next stage in the process.

By now I have completed a thorough inspection of the wing and worked on it for perhaps half an hour. I know the wing, I know its strengths and weaknesses and if I have made the right choice it can now be repaired in one go.

You can see the damaged area from the photograph. I was going to take a photo of the lump of glass matting which was the previous repair, but I did not want to teach you any bad habits!

Mount the wing in some sort of holding frame, or clamp it to something. There is nothing worse than chasing a wing along the garage floor while trying to repair it.

Get out the grinder, the tin snips or any other tool you use to cut steel. *NOT* a hammer and chisel. From now on we want accuracy and no distortion.

On a job like this I would cut round the rusty hole with tin snips. There is plenty of room for them and you can get a nice clean cut. Make sure you cut out all the rot. Even a few small holes on the edge of your cut can cause problems later on, so do a thorough job.

Having cut the rot out, grind the edges smooth and straight with the grinder. While the grinder is still on, clean off any paint or underseal from both sides of the wing within half an inch from the cut. This will make welding easier and prevent dangerous paint fumes.

For the next stage you need a sheet of card, an old pair of scissors and a sharp pencil.

Hold the sheet of card against the hole in the wing and trace around the edge with the pencil. Make sure this is done accurately, otherwise you will have to do it again.

Our project front wing as collected from the scrap yard. The glass fibre patch has been removed, leaving this ugly mess.

The damaged area marked out with a pencil. Make sure you cut back to clean, sound, rust-free steel, otherwise you will hit problems when welding.

Cut out the damaged area with tin snips. This job would be easier if the wing was up on a bench or table.

When you have traced round, cut out the shape with the scissors.

Offer up the cardboard template to the wing. What you want is the cardboard to sit inside the boundaries of the hole with about one sixteenth inch all round. If you don't achieve this first time try again. Card is cheap!

Get this stage exactly right, then mark 'outside' or 'inside' or any other suitable mark which you understand to identify which way the card sits in the hole. Don't laugh! I have been caught out numerous times by cutting out my card then dropping it or somehow turning it upside down. When I complete the next stage I find it does not fit properly.

You may have already worked out the next stage. Lay the card on a flat piece of steel which will be the repair patch. Now, mark round the outline of the card with your pencil. Again, make sure it is done accurately. The better the fit at this stage, the neater will be the final repair.

Cut out the steel with tin snips or other cutting tool. Cut close to the marked line to ensure an accurate fit. Don't think you can file bits off to make it fit. This is like chasing your tail — you will only open up one gap too wide and will have to throw away the patch and start again. Get it right — get it accurate.

Once it is cut out, offer it up to the wing. If you have done everything right it will be a nice neat fit, with just one sixteenth inch all round. The next step is to clamp it in position.

For this I would use my Inter-grip welding clamps. You can use Mole welding clamps if the patch is not too far fronm the edge of the wing, or devise another method yourself. If you are really stuck, use some little scraps of steel and self-tapping screws. A plate and two screws at each end of the patch will do okay, and you can fill in the holes later bv 'Blobbing.'

Cut through the outer, folded over edge with a junior hacksaw. Just cut enough to sever the crimped edge – no more.

Right, patch in place and we have been working for perhaps an hour. Time for a coffee. I say this because I want you to stop and think. Go over each step to check that everything has been done properly, because the next step is the welding.

For this I am going to use my number 1 tip, and a low pressure. I cannot tell you what the pressure is because I find that the Portapak is not all that accurate at low pressures.

Get the goggles on, have some one six-teenth inch filler rod ready and light the torch. Gently heat one corner of the patch AND the wing. When it is up to welding temperature add some filler rod and make a tack weld. Repeat this process on the other corners. When the tacks are in place, remove the welding clamps or other fix-ings.

If the wing has a lot of shape, gently tap the patch into the correct shape. Remember that you are going to run a small layer of plastic filler over the final job, so the patch wants to be below the level of the wing rather than above it.

Use the 'Leap-frogging' method of welding described elsewhere in the book, and complete the weld. You want to weld all round the patch to complete the job.

During the welding, stop and hammer the welds down. When I say hammer, I don't mean swinging a sledge-hammer, I mean tap with just enough force to achieve the desired result. What you are doing is flat-tening the welds while they are hot. This strengthens them and saves time with the grinder.

When welding is complete, grind off the welds to smooth them. Use your eye and your fingers to decide how much to grind, but remember grinding makes steel HOT!

When the grinding is complete I would go over the area, on both sides of the wing,

The new piece of steel clamped in position with Inter-grip clamps. The lower, curved part of the panel will be formed as I weld.

This is what you are left with when all the rot is cut away. The inner support needs a little work as it is rusty. Do this before adding the new section.

First, tack weld then remove the clamps. When everything is fitted correctly, weld the new section in place. The curved part of the wing was formed with the help of the tool shown. It provides a pattern for curves and is used by carpet-fitters and tile-fitters.

with a rotating wire brush. This should remove all the remaining paint and dirt from the patch area.

When this is done, scratch the area with the end of a screwdriver or an old file. This will provide an extra 'key' for the skim of plastic filler.

As soon as this is done, paint on some primer paint. I use Comma Stoprust which is as good as anything and available in Halfords. Make sure the paint gets into all the corners.

If you have followed the text closely and studied the photographs, you should have a tidy repair which will last another 20 years if properly protected.

Our exercise wing is now looking good. You have spent perhaps one or two hours so far and the biggest job is done.

Round the headlamp hole is still looking a bit ragged but I want to leave that until the wing is back on the car. As mentioned previously, to repair the headlamp you need a headlamp retaining ring (or similar part for your particular car) and probably a plastic headlamp bowl. When all this is put together you have a cheap, tidy wing for a fraction of what it could have cost you.

Just for the record, I have a brand new Ford wing which I paid £90 for. I'm told that if a new batch is made they could cost from £120 upwards EACH. So you have saved a lot of money which can be spent somewhere else on the restoration.

The two main tools used for the repair. A cardboard template cut to match the damaged area, and the contour tool. It can be made to copy any curve. I took the 'good' contour from another wing, then used the shape to form the welded section.

A modern Ford Fiesta suffering from wheel arch rot. This car was repaired by 'cheap and cheerful' brazing on a new section. The rot will return in a few years – or less.

Wheel Arch Repairs

Under this heading I will include fitting wide arches to cover fat tyres. These extra wide wheel arches can be quite simple, like those available for Minis, where it is a moulded plastic assembly which bolts or pop-rivets onto the existing bodywork.

The job I want to discuss is fitting a new wheel arch repair section. Rear wheel arch sections are available for many cars and consist of a sheet of steel stamped to the shape of the wheel arch. This shape is quite complicated if you look at it closely, so these sections can often be cut up and used for much smaller, localised repair jobs.

Don't forget that you have to weld or fix TWO edges of the repair panel to the car. The outer, or upper surface is welded to the outside of the rear quarter panel. However, most people forget that there is an inner wheel arch which must be welded to the inner, lower lip on the repair panel. This takes the time and adds hours to the job. Believe me, it's no fun trying to weld inside a wheel arch, above your head!

If you are going to fit one, remember that the biggest problem is distortion, as you are welding a large flat area of unsupported steel which is called the rear quarter panel.

There are several photographs showing the sequence of events in the Cortina Restoration section later in the book. Let me talk you through some of the important points now.

Hold the repair section against the car and mark a line to cut to. You have to decide if you are going to use a butt joint or an overlap joint. You may also want to consider a joggle joint. Butt is difficult to do without distortion, overlap needs more bodyfiller and could allow water into the join, while joggle needs a lot of extra work to make the step. I can't advise you on this. You will have to make your own decision. (I know some people use an overlap joint and braze these sections in place).

I chose to use a butt joint, so cut my rear quarter panel accordingly. I cut off the old steel with tin snips, and tried the new panel for fit. It needed a little bit of adjustment at the front edge, where it meets the C post. Once it was located properly, I took it all off again, and made repairs to the inner wheel arch, which folds over and meets the outer wheel arch.

This took a couple of hours, and involved a lot of cutting of 'V's to get the curves right. Remember to check for fire hazards, such as paint, bitumen sealer or soft trim, before lighting the torch. Often the rear quarter panel will have large sound-deadening pads stuck to the inside, and this can start a nasty fire.

When the inner wheel arch repairs are completed, offer up the outer arch again. If everything still fits, clamp it in position. I used Inter-grip clamps for this plus some Mole grips at either end. I tack welded, then hammered the welds, all the time checking that the panels were not losing their correct shape or contours. Then I welded a bit here, and a bit there, jumping about the join line until all was welded. I also alternated between welding the outside join and the inner join to the inner wheel arch. I did create some distortion, which I believe was unavoidable because of the way I tackled the job. Perhaps I should have brazed it. Anyway, I have done two wheel arches now, and both have needed some filler to finish them off.

REAR CORNER REPAIR

These repair sections consist of the lower, rear corner of the rear quarter panel and are available for many older cars. They are fairly easy to fit, especially on the Cortina as they blend into the styled contour or 'lump' which blends into the rear bumper. The repair panel welds into the lower part of this lump and helps to disguise the join.

Once again the procedure is, examine, measure, cut, clean up, offer up then clamp. When you have done all that, you can tack weld, then weld using the 'leap-

A Cortina with a rotten wheel arch cut away, ready to have the inner wheel arch repaired. (See the Cortina Restoration feature for more photographs.)

Two new wheel arch repair panels ready to be fitted. These panels take more time to fit that you expect, due to inner wheel arch rot.

frog' technique. I don't believe you will have much difficulty with this sort of job as long as you take your time.

I got caught out on one of my cars, as the above-mentioned 'lump' consisted of glass fibre. Once this started to burn I discovered the whole area had been expertly repaired sometime in the past. I had no idea it was there.

I hope I have given you some ideas for working on outer panels in this Chapter. The keys to success are planning and pati-

ence, and a low welding temperature. If you want to restore or 'hot rod' you will have to pay extra attention to outer panels to achieve the sort of finish which turns heads and gathers crowds.

Louvres used to be difficult to make. Not now. These beautiful louvres were made from a simple hardwood tool, available from Russell's Motor Services.

Loose rust and holes indicate work required. Outer panels are seen by everyone, so take time and effort to get them right.

This Capri has had a new patch panel fitted behind the B post. This panel was made by the author, but 'custom' repair panels are available from the Consul Capri Owner's Club.

Doors And Hoods _____

Rusty or damaged doors can mar the appearance of any car. The stick-on stripe on this car served as a guideline for repairs, as all the rust was below the line. The dent was simply filled with plastic filler.

Doors are complex assemblies which can spoil the look of an otherwise perfect car. If the door does not hang correctly, it will show up straight away, and every time you try to open or shut it, you will curse it. As well as the metalwork on the door, there are other areas which have to be restored, such as the rubber beading round the edge of the door. This serves three main purposes:

1) To keep the water out,

2) To keep the outside noises out,

3) To provide flexibility in the fitting of the door to the door frame. If the door is not exactly right, then the rubber will accommodate it to some extent.

Before we start to look at repairing doors, I want to pass on a tip about removing doors. This will help you to remove and refit a door single-handed.

Get hold of an axle stand and place it under the edge of the door when the it is in the open position, now wind down the window.

Having removed any trim you have to, mark the hinge positions with a pencil or sharp screwdriver. This will allow you to refit them in the exact same position.

Now, loosen off the bolts which hold the hinge to the door – NOT the one holding the hinge to the A post. You will find you can support the door with one hand, and loosen the bolts with the other. The door will continue to hang until all but one of the bolts is undone. Leave a top bolt till last. The door will be held by the top bolt, but its own weight will locate it against the bottom hinge. If you remove the top bolts first, the weight of the door would then make the door rotate towards the ground. Think about it. Finally, loosen the top bolt, while steadying the door. I find I can put my shoulder through the window and support the top of the door with my shoulder. The door will rotate towards the

axle stand and stay supported on that until the bolt is removed.

Anyone of reasonable strength should be able to remove and fit a door with the help of the axle stand. I've done it dozens of times. Re-hanging the door is a little more difficult, so if you need help, ask for it. I have worked out a method to do this too. Again, it involves supporting the top of the door on your shoulder (you put your shoulder through the window from the inside outwards) and locating the door on the hinges again. Move the door hinges so that they are in the open position. Now lift the door onto the hinges. Luckily, many cars have a mixture of bolts and studs, so the door will hang on the studs till you get a few bolts on. Occasionally you find a problem when the hinge folds shut, leaving you still holding the door. If this happens you have no choice but to start again.

This method may not suit everyone, but I frequently use it as I have had to work on

A close up of the rusty doors shown in the previous picture. Both of these doors can be saved by patching. For rust as bad as this, check that the door frame is sound, because it may have suffered over the years.

Ooops! This is accident damage, which is not covered by this book. However the steel looks sound and the damage should straighten with hammer and dolly work. (Photo by Mark Hill).

my own most of the time. If you are at all worried about holding the weight of a door, then seek help. It will only take your assistant a few minutes to help you.

Door Repairs

There are only three choices available when it comes to doors:

1) Outright replacement with a better door from another car,

2) Replacement with a brand new door (if one is available),

3) Replacement or repair of the outer part of the door known as the door skin.

Let's have a quick look at replacing the complete door, before spending more time on the other two choices.

If you are lucky enough to find a brand new door for your car, the chances are it will be finished in some sort of primer. You'll be very lucky if you find a door in the correct colour scheme for your car! So you know right from the start that you will have to have the door painted. After that is established the other main points to look at are:

1) Is the replacement door EXACTLY the same as the original? Even minor differences can cause you problems later when you try to fit it.

2) Does the replacement door have all the correct fittings, such as locks, handles, window winders and so on. If not, do you have the correct items available and *DO THEY FIT?*

3) Is the door new? What I mean is, has someone else repaired this door and is now trying to pass it off as new? Run a magnet over the door surface to try to detect any plastic body filler. Better still, remove the interior trim from the door and have a look inside. Very few people are going to disguise a repair on the inside of the door.

If the door is not exactly what you want, are you satisfied that you can modify it to suit your car. If you are not completely sure, then walk away and look elsewhere.

Door Hanging

Having established that the door is completely suitable, let's have a look at door hanging. This used to be an art in itself, and even today it can take a lot of time and skill to get a mass-produced door to fit a mass-produced bodyshell.

There are four edges to a door, so there are four main problem areas for a bad fit:

1) The front edge of the door. This can be adjusted on the hinge (that is the car side of the hinge) and on the door. What you are trying to achieve is a fit which lines up neatly and smoothly with the rear edge of the front wing. So, there is little point spending time getting this part right if the wing is damaged in any way.

2) The rear edge of the door. This edge has to follow the contours of either the 'B' Post (the name given to the pillar in the middle of a 4-door car which carries the hinge for the rear doors) or the contours of the rear wing if it is a rear door. In both cases the rear edge of the door carries some sort of mechanism to hold the door shut, and this must be adjusted properly to prevent people falling out. Don't laugh! At least one British Ford showed this problem when door striker plates wore excessively.

3) The top edge of the door. This edge has to follow the contours of the roof line or gutter line of the car. It can be adjusted by the hinges on the door post and on the door itself.

4) The bottom edge of the door. This edge has to follow the contour of the sill or kick plate. It can be adjusted by the hinges on the door post and on the door itself.

Now, it may seem that I am stating the obvious. This is for a purpose. When fitting doors, and things start to go wrong, it is amazing how quickly people forget what they are trying to do. The previous four notes outline what you are doing when setting up a door.

Remember too that if you set up the top edge, the bottom edge may stick out (or in) or if you set the front edge exactly, the rear edge may not be right. In the end it is a compromise. It does not help if there is a fault on the door as you will never get a distorted door to fit.

It is possible to put a wooden block between the door frame and the 'A' or 'B' Post of the car and shut the door on the block. This can occasionally open up a small gap and finalise the adjustment. Be careful if you do this. You can exert a lot of pressure by this method so think long and hard before you try it.

Now, as I promised at the start of the Chapter we will spend a lot more time describing how you can repair a door cheaply. First, changing a door skin.

Right, the bodywork of this 1955 Pontiac is generally in excellent condition, but the rust above and below the back headlamp will mean some neat welding will be required. (Photo by Terry Hill).

A 1950 Nash Ambassador shows a bonnet (or hood) with a definite shape to it. This example looks as though it could be saved, showing very few signs of age. (Photo by Terry Hill).

New Door Skins

The first golden rule is, never fit a new skin on a distorted or damaged door, otherwise the new skin will simple 'set' the distortion for ever. So before you lift a tool, make sure the door fits properly. As I said right at the start of the book, we are dealing with rust damage or minor parking scars, NOT with accident damage which is an entirely separate subject. If the door is damaged due to an accident, seek professional help.

a) Having established that the door is not distorted, and that it fits well, mark all the positions of the hinges with a scriber or sharp screwdriver. This will help the refitting process.

b) Remove the door from the car.

c) Check that the replacement skin is correct by test fitting it over the original door. Check if door lock holes, door handle holes and so on are already in the door skin or if you have to drill these later.

d) Remove all interior trim from the door. This will prevent damage to the trim and lessen the risk of you setting fire to plastic trim. When you are entirely sure that the new skin will fit, start to remove the old skin as follows:

A correctly fitted hood enhances any restored car. This beautiful Ford Capri was photographed at a rally near Lancaster a few years ago.

The boot lid (or trunk lid) is also a perfect fit. Only some 16,000 Capris were built, sharing a lot of the same mechanical parts as the Cortina. They are very distinctive cars.

The best tool for this is an angle-grinder. Nothing else is quite as good, so try to borrow, hire or buy one before starting this job. Grind round the OUTER edges where the skin is folded over the edge of the door. This way you have to remove the minimum of metal and there is less risk of damaging the door frame. You will find that the job does not take long to do. Remember, you MUST wear goggles and protective gloves when using an angle-grinder.

e) Once you have ground all the accessible edges, you will probably have to use the hammer and chisel to release some spot welds holding the skin to the door. Do this as gently as possible.

f) Remove the door skin. It will probably come away in one piece, but beware any sharp edges left from the grinding. At this point you will probably discover that the door frame will need some minor attention. If it needs a major re-work, then you had better brush-up your inspection technique. Anyway, repairing a door frame is not too difficult, as all the work is hidden!

I prefer to use small repair sections if I have to repair a door frame. Remember to remove any rubber sealing strips along the bottom of the door. These can burn quite readily, and the fumes they give off are very unpleasant. Better to remove the seal and be prepared to re-stick it when the job is done.

Cut out a section of rust and repair it with new steel. Cut out another section and repair it, until the job is completed. Don't let too much heat build up otherwise you might encourage distortion. You will probably find that all the rust damage is along the bottom edge, with the worst of it near the front.

Once you have repaired the frame, it is best if you try it again on the car. As I said before, if you fix the new skin over a distorted frame, it will be distorted forever.

g) When you are satisfied that the frame is perfect, smooth off the welding on the frame repairs with the angle grinder.

Now it is time to fit the new skin. Place the door on some matting or old carpet on the floor. This packing will avoid damage if the door moves during the work. Offer the skin up to the door. If all is well the skin should be a push fit onto the door. When you are sure it is fitting all round you have a choice of what to do next.

Some authorities recommend you make a few spot welds to locate the door skin to the door frame. This will prevent any movement during the hammer and dolly stage. However, I can't see any great advantage to this and the do-it-yourself man runs the risk of distorting the new skin. So

A very rare 1954 Studebaker Commander, showing a lot of surface rust on the trunk lid and roof. Much of this damage has been caused by bird droppings, but should be restorable with a little effort and a new paint job. (Photo by Terry Hill).

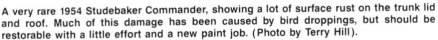

This Capri door has been welded on the bottom of the door frame. The rubber seal along the edges will have to be replaced later.

I suggest you go on to the hammer and dolly stage next.

Using a good panel hammer and a dolly with a straight edge, tap the fixing edge of the door skin over the frame. Start at one end of, say, the bottom edge and move along, tapping the edge of the skin with the hammer while the dolly supports the outside of the skin (on the outside surface of the door). Make sure the dolly is clean, and does not have any lumps of underseal left from previous jobs. If there are any lumps, they will be imprinted on the surface of the door skin.

Continue this process until the door skin is held in place. Don't worry if you have to go round the edge a few times. Better to tap it into place gently and take your time than bash it into place and risk a mistake.

You should find that the skin edge will fold right over and can be hammered down on the inside of the door frame. Go round again gently to make sure every part is hammered down.

On some cars you need to put a few spot welds near the top, for example where the skin meets a glass frame. Treat this carefully as too much heat will cause distor-

tion. Remember to remove any felt or plastic guide strips (next to the glass), which may melt or ignite when you weld.

If all has gone well, you should now have a perfect door. By doing it yourself you have saved a lot of cash which can be invested in another part of the car.

Door Skin Repairs

In some ways the next part of this Chapter is the hardest; repairing an existing door skin. You would have to do this if a new door skin is not available. This is very often the case, and I have had to repair doors on all three of my Fords.

This dealer offers a tremendous variety of Cortina spares. Although specialising in the Lotus Cortina variant, many parts will also suit other models in the Cortina range.

Generally the rust forms at the front corner of the door. Sometimes there is rust at the rear corner, and if the door has really been neglected, the entire lower length of the door skin can be pitted with holes. Quite often this is due to blocked drain holes in the bottom of the door. Water runs down the glass and gets trapped in the bottom of the door along with some mud, dirt and any other debris. Rust is the result. So before I forget to tell you, remember to keep all the drain holes along the bottom of the door clear of blockages. All you need to do is occasionally stick a small screwdriver up into each hole. This will dislodge any debris which should then fall out all over your hand! Better that than a rusty door.

For the actual repairs, I prefer to remove the door to repair it, although there is no law which says you must. In some cases it might be better to leave the door on the car. That would certainly help your door hanging problem! I would suggest to you that it is much easier to repair a door if it is fixed firmly to something, or laid out on a bench. Trying to repair a door propped against a wall is not always satisfactory.

Using the angle grinder, or a lot of hard work with a blow lamp or paint stripper,

remove the paint and underseal from the lower three or four inches of the door. This is the time when you want to discover the extent of the rust. Clean all the paint off and have a scrape with a screwdriver. When you are absolutely sure you have found all the rust holes, decide how to patch the door. Will one patch be okay? Will it be better to use a small patch on each corner? Do you feel confident about running a patch right along the bottom of the door?

When you have answered the questions and decided a course of action, get the tin snips and the panel steel out. Get a piece of cardboard and cut out a cardboard repair section. REMEMBER that on the bottom edge of the patch (the bit that will form the bottom of the door) you will have to allow another half inch for the fold-over. Similarly, allow a half inch fold-over if the patch forms part of the front edge of the door. When you get this right, cut out the rusty section from the door. You can use tin snips, or any other kind of panel cutter. What you do not want is distortion.

The front corner of the Capri door has been patched and hammer welded. Some more work is needed before this job becomes an invisible mend!

Cut out the rusty section but do not throw it away yet. Place the cardboard cut-out over the hole in the door and check the fit. If all is well start to trace the shape onto steel. Scribe this on the steel. If all is not well, make a new cardboard template using the edges of the cut out hole.

When you have the steel repair section cut out, check the shape of the door. You will find that you have a flat repair section and a curved door panel. You will have to bend the patch to match the shape in the door. Generally, there is not a lot of shape, but unless you get it right it will buckle when you weld. I use my knee, the rim of a tyre — in fact anything to hand which has the approximate shape. Constantly measure the patch against the door. Aim to have a patch with a gap of one sixteenth of an inch smaller than the hole. (Don't forget the parts which fold over the door frame need to be half an inch larger than the hole!) When you are sure you have got it right go on to the next step.

Fit the repair section into position and locate it with welding clamps, or whatever fixing method you have available. For a job like this, I would reach for my trusty Inter-grip welding clamps.

With the patch firmly in place, make a last inspection before lighting the torch. If everything looks all right, make a few tack welds round the patch.

Allow these to cool, then remove the welding clamps, otherwise they may get trapped between the patch and the door skin. This is because of distortion during welding.

Now weld an inch or so on one side of the patch, followed by some hammer and dolly work. Alternate between welding and hammering, and you will achieve a nice neat finish. It may be difficult to get the dolly into the correct position, and it often pays to try fitting the dolly before welding. If the dolly does fit into the door frame, be careful when hammering, as hot debris will almost certainly burn an unprotected hand. An old leather glove is great for this sort of work.

When you have done your best with the welding torch and hammer, run the angle grinder over the welds to smooth down anything missed by the hammer and dolly, then run a thin layer of plastic filler over the repair to finish it off. Prime and paint for an invisible mend!

You can apply these tips to corner patches or full length patches. Be careful if you decide to run a full length patch along the bottom edge of the door. You run a big risk of distorting the entire door skin. The reason is that the whole door skin is a large, unsupported area, so the chances of distortion are much greater. Some authorities recommend a joggle joint for this sort of job, and I would not disagree with this

I have welded this patch onto the door skin, but have not completed the job. The patch has still to be folded over the door frame. That's the problem working outdoors — it rains!

approach. You may also want to consider butt welding the job, then hammering the weld down over a grooved shrinking dolly. This would sink the weld, pull both metal parts together and help to reduce any distortion. Note my use of the word 'help'. I don't think anyone would disagree if I said have this job done professionally if you are in any doubt about it. Shoddy doors will be noticed by everyone, and while you might find this acceptable for a drive to work car, it would certainly not be acceptable for a car restored to a higher standard.

Before I leave doors, just a final word about making sure you have the correct door skin for your car. I have noticed in several repair panel catalogues that there are often two different door skins for the same car. This may be due to things like a change in door handles, or the fitting of a new type of door lock. Either way, be very careful when you order a door skin. Make absolutely sure that you get the correct item. If it does not suit, send it back. Don't get yourself in the position where you have stripped off the old skin while waiting on the new one to arrive. That is fatal. IF the new one is not available any more, IF the new one does not fit, IF the new one does not arrive when it was supposed to, you are going to look pretty silly with a doorframe and no skin. I think it is Murphy's Law which states that 'If a thing can go wrong, then it will' and this is an ideal situation to test the theory.

Don't remove any metalwork from a car until:

A later view of the above job. The edge has been folded over and tapped down with hammer and dolly. A patch on the bottom of the door frame is just being welded. The clamp is holding the rubber seal clear of the welding area.

This tip is so obvious now, but it took me weeks to think of it! That dummy speaker grill covers a ragged hole in the interior trim, left by the previous owner ripping his loudspeaker out! It will help keep the car tidy until I can get a new trim panel.

1) You have the new part available and you know it will fit, or

2) You know exactly what you have to do to make a new part.

I speak from experience...

When you have fitted your new door skin, and come to replace the handles, locks and so on, don't damage the skin by sloppy use of tools. A slipped screwdriver, an overtightened spanner or a wandering twist drill could cause a crease or gouge in your new door. If you need to drill holes in the door skin, or in any other body panel, try this tip. Instead of marking the point for the hole on the steel, stick a bit of sticky tape on the steel first. Then mark on the tape, then drill through the tape. The tape helps to locate the drill bit and prevent it 'walking' along the panel. It is better still if you gently use a small centre punch to mark the intended hole.

Now that all the dire warnings are out of the way, we'll have a look at tailgates before moving on to bonnets and boots.

Estate Tailgates

Big estate rear doors or tailgates can be expensive items to replace if they rust out. I've seen many Volvo estates (particularly the 145 model) with badly rusted tailgates. Luckily there are repair panels available for this job.

The repair sections I've seen consist of two parts. You might be lucky and just need one. One part is the outer skin, which forms the part of the tailgate below the numberplate, the other is a tailgate frame bottom. This is, as its name suggests, a new frame assembly for the bottom of the tailgate and it goes underneath the skin.

Examine your rusty tailgate, and have a prod with a sharp screwdriver. If you are sure that the tailgate frame is sound, just order the skin. If you have bigger problems, then you will need the frame as well.

Decide how you are going to fix the new skin in position. You will have to weld it along its top surface, or overlap and pop rivet, or joggle the lower edge of the old tailgate, or whatever other method you can figure out. I would be tempted to butt weld this job, but I could be persuaded to use the joggler to put a step in the top panel, so that the lower repair panel would fit flush. Decide what you are going to do,

because this will affect the decision about where to cut.

Either way, you will have to cut the old skin off. Mark where to cut, using the new outer skin as a template.

When you have cut the rusty part out, offer up the new skin to check the fit. If you have measured and cut accurately, you should have a close-fitting repair panel. Clamp the repair panel in position and carefully check all the measurements. It is best if you can refit the tailgate (if you removed it) or try to shut it with the new panel in place. Shutting it will give you the best chance to check for misalignment of the panel.

When you are satisfied everything is all right, weld the panel in place. I would 'leapfrog' this job as well, and this technique is well described in other parts of this book.

If the main frame of the tailgate is rusted out, you will have to butt joint the repair panel to the old panel. Make sure you have removed all the rusty steel from the old panel, otherwise your problem will just re-occur.

How would you like to have to sort this lot out? A 1940 Pontiac, it is described as too far gone to restore, but might prove a useful source of spare parts. (Photo by Terry Hill).

If all else fails, then have a look in the local scrapyards for a replacement tailgate. Remember it may be cheaper to buy one which needs just the outer repair panel, if your original was so bad it needed inside and outside repairs. You will have to weigh up all the pros and cons of a particular situation. I'm sorry I can't help any more.

Hoods

I wasn't sure how to title this section. Most European readers will recognise bonnet rather than hood, but hood is somehow a more descriptive name. Anyway, whatever you call it, we are talking about the outer body panel which normally goes at the front of the car and covers the engine.

As usual, hoods come in all sorts of shapes and sizes. The older, traditional hood was in two pieces, with a great big hinge along the top. You could lift open one side of the hood at a time. Later cars used one-piece hoods, which tended to have a lot of shape. Later still hoods got flatter and contained less shape becoming large almost flat panels.

Older designs used louvres, and I have already shown you how to create louvres

quite cheaply. Newer designs sometimes feature 'power bulges' which are really bulges in the hood to accommodate carburettors or some similar component which does not quite fit in the hole where the engine goes.

Anyway, how do you repair or restore a hood? I'll have to split the answer into two parts — the old style hoods and the new style hoods. Let's look at the old style hoods first.

You will probably find it much easier to restore an old style hood rather than a newer one. The reason is simple. Steel was used much thicker in days gone by. Unless you have been very unfortunate and your hood has spent twenty years in the river, you should have something which will clean up and repair quite readily.

If repairs are needed, it is usually a question of cutting out a part of the hood, and welding in a new piece. This procedure has already been covered in previous Chapters.

Make sure that the hood is not distorted before welding, as you might run the risk of setting the distortion into the panel for good with the welding torch. Check the fit of the hood before you carry out repairs.

The only exception to this would be where the hood was in a flimsy condition, and fitting and re-fitting might cause more damage. Sometimes a hood will appear flimsy because one or two welds have broken away. This can cause the whole assembly to flex and give rise to fears that the hood is beyond repair. Look out for broken welds when examining your hood. Also examine the condition of any supporting stays, or hinge brackets. A few broken welds in these places can cause the whole assembly to temporarily lose its shape. If you cannot repair a hinge assembly you may be able to find a second hand one in either the scrapyard or from the Owners Club.

New Hoods

Repairing new-style, flat hoods is much more difficult than working the traditional type. The reason is that designers have used double thickness steel for the hood. Two very thin sheets can literally be stuck or glued together to make a much stronger assembly. The problem is if one thickness rusts, you have trouble trying to work on the rusty bit without damaging the other piece.

If you have a rusty hood, I would first of all look around to see what was available second hand (or new!). What I am suggesting is that you examine the options for replacement first, before considering any repairs.

In other Chapters I have discussed various parts of the car which are noticed more than others. Hoods come very high on this list. It is at the front of the car, where everyone looks, and it is high up and in full view. You must get it neat and tidy.

Prices for second hand hoods will vary enormously. I have seen brand new Cortina hoods for £5, while I have been asked to pay £15 for a second hand hood in a scrapyard. Here's a tip to remember. I went into a yard and found an almost mint condition front hood for my Capri. The yard owner wanted £15. I said sorry, too much, and went away. The following week I was back for some other parts, and it was a different man taking the money. I asked about the Capri hood and he said £5. So I took it. I consider that to be an honest deal. However sometimes you are offered a deal like this where the cash goes straight into the assistant's pocket. I don't like dealing that way but you may consider it acceptable.

Anyway, find out about new or second hand hoods before considering repairs.

I have some rust underneath my hood. It is near the fixing catch — the bit that holds the hood shut against the top of the front panel. I believe this area can be repaired, as it occurs at the point where the front of the hood curves the most. The inner skin does not curve the same way, so in effect the inner skin bridges the outer skin. This bit can be cut or ground away, and a new piece made up and welded in. You may need to use a flat chisel to get between the two skins of metal. Remember that any work like this on the underside of the hood — if it involves welding — will almost certainly burn the paint on the outer surface. Don't think you will get away with repairs and no painting. Sorry, but you won't.

Although there is a lot of rust around the headlamp of this 1955 Pontiac, the hood looks to be in good condition. Have a good look on the inside of the hood before handing over cash!

This trunk lid from a 1948 Studebaker might be better than your rusty example. Somebody, somewhere, wants it! Apart from the tatty paintwork, which will need rubbing down to bare metal, the lid looks basically sound. Before you pay, find out if you can still get a key for the lock, otherwise you could have problems ... (Photo by Terry Hill).

The original hood catch has been removed, and quick-release pins fitted to this Cortina. Note the rubber wedges on either side of the wing edges. These help stop vibration. You can just see signs of a neat welding job on the left hand MacPherson strut-top panel.

Hood Fitting

Generally there is not a lot of sideways adjustment on a hood. The hinges are often welded to the inner wing and can't be adjusted. This simplifies hood fitting.

On the Cortina hood (which is fairly typical) there are four bolts which hold the hood to the hinges. These bolts can be loosened, and the hood moved relative to the hinges. This allows some adjustment to be made. I like to mark a pencil line round the hinge where it meets the hood, before I remove the hood. This at least gives you a starting point for adjustment. You may also be able to use a rust line which often forms in the same place!

Loosen the bolts and get the hood in what you think is the right position. Gently tighten one bolt on each side. Now shut the hood and examine the fit. If it needs to go forwards or backwards, you may be able to push it in the required direction without opening it again. If the bolts are just tight enough to hold the position, but just slack enough to allow adjustment, then you will quickly achieve a good fit.

Remember that hoods are often supported by little rubber blocks along the sides. These often fit into the top of the inner

This second hand trunk lid cost just £5 a few years ago. I knew it would not be painted properly for a few years, so I gave it a protective coat of Comma Stoprust which has fended off the weather quite well.

wing. If yours are missing – get some new ones. They won't cost much, and can improve the fit of the hood and prevent vibration and drumming.

Finally, before I leave hoods, can I remind you that a lot of noise can be reduced by fitting a sound-deadening kit to the underside of the hood. Generally this consists of thick felt which is glued or otherwise fixed to the underneath of the hood. It cuts down a lot of engine noise and can make for a more comfortable journey. Ask around to see if there is a kit for your car.

If you have any quick release fixings for the hood, such as rubber clips or spikes with split pins, you MUST be sure that they are secure. A hood with hinges at the back will be totally wrecked if it tries to open at speed. The wind will rip it open, twist it and possibly cause damage to the windscreen and anyone in the car. Don't take any chances with this sort of thing. Generally there is a safety catch on hoods which provides a 'second chance' if the hood does open. Make sure this still works after you have removed, repaired or re-placed a hood.

Boot Lids

Most of what has been said about hoods can equally be applied to boot lids. Sometimes you will be able to repair a boot lid but you often face the double skin problem.

I suggest you look for a replacement before you try repairs. If you do try repairs then you will find enough information throughout this book to tell you what to do.

Remember that boot lids almost always have some sort of rubber seal round them. If you want to keep the floor of the boot dry – and rust-free – then you need to keep the seal in good condition. Read the monthly magazines for specialists in rubber seals. A few pounds spent now on a new seal could save hundreds in a few years if you have to start rebuilding the boot floor as I had to do in a previous Chapter.

If you do change the boot lid, don't forget to check the lock before you slam it shut! Try the key in the lock and ensure it works properly otherwise you are going to look pretty foolish trying to get help opening your new boot lid.

Sound deadening material on the underside of the boot lid may help to reduce drumming which can occur if the lid vibrates at a certain speed. This is called resonance and can cause discomfort if it annoys too much. A few strips of adhesive material can make all the difference. Ask at your motor factors or accessory shop.

Doors and hoods don't come much more basic than this! As I recall, it is a 1929 Citroen which was offered for sale recently. This is another good opportunity to remind you about 'shape' in body panels ...

Sliding doors are fitted to this early 1950s Morris Commercial van. Panel repairs consisted of replacing the lower edges on both doors, plus a small welding job on the sturdy chassis. That 3-speed gearbox was terrible, though!

I hope I have been able to pass on something useful about hoods, tailgates and boot lids in this Chapter. In the next Chapter I will show you ways to protect the metalwork you have worked so hard to restore.

The lower edge of a Morris Minor door is a sure candidate for rust. This example could probably survive a bit longer, but more expensive repairs would then be needed. Repairs consist of welding in new made-to-measure repair panels.

A 1968 Pontiac Parisienne with 327 cubic inch motor showing some signs of accident and rust damage. Refurbishing work has started—the hood has been repaired and primered, but there are still a lot of minor jobs to do. (Photo by Terry Hill).

The tailgate on this 1980 Pontiac Safari station wagon is showing signs of early rust along the lower edge. It looks as though it can be treated without welding, but if not repaired now, will deteriorate rapidly. Rust in the surrounding panels looks more serious. (Photo by Mark Hill).

Paint And Protect

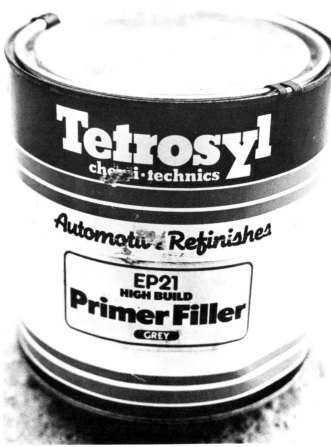

Paint protects and decorates your metalwork. Good preparation is the key to success, as paint will not hide problem bodywork. A good quality primer or undercoat is essential to a good paint job.

When you have finished all the bodywork repairs and restoration on your car it is time to start the process known as 're-finishing.' This means that you flatten out any remaining dents, fill any dips, smooth off all the remaining paintwork and prepare for re-painting.

Painting is a major subject in itself and there are a number of specialist books on the market already which do a very good job of explaining this complicated subject. Although not listed separately in the Bibliography section, I recommend Miles Wilkins' 'How to Restore Paintwork', which is number four in Osprey's restoration series.

Finishing a Dent

When you have completed all the hammer and dolly work on a dent, run a body file over the repaired area. If you have a special body file, move it along the panel in one direction, then again at right angles to the first movement. This X-pattern will show up any high spots in the panel. (A high spot is an area of the panel which stands out above the correct level of the bodywork.). The body file will show up high spots by making them shiny where the file removes a small amount of metal. Low areas will not be touched by the file and will remain dirty or painted.

If there are any high spots, they will have to be tapped down using hammer and dolly. You MUST finish all the metal to the correct contour or lower.

Using Plastic Filler

Plastic body filler used to have a bad reputation, back in the days when the product was new and the craftsman didn't know the correct technique. Nowadays, the product is superb, never gives any trouble and can be applied by anyone with a little common sense.

First of all, let's establish some basic rules about the use of plastic filler:

1) Repairs to steel panels must always be finished off as well as time or money will allow.

2) Plastic fillers are only used to finish the repair.

3) Plastic fillers allow the novice to create a perfect, smooth panel with just a bit of effort.

Plastic fillers are NOT for:

Idiots who lump it on in an effort to hide major dents, OR for any areas which are structural — that is any part of the car which relies on strength for safety.

Things were so bad a number of years ago I saw a magazine article where a rear chassis leg was repaired (rather, the rusty leg was filled) with plastic filler, smoothed off, painted and presented for a safety test. Hopefully this practice has now ceased, and magazines are more responsible in what they print. A botch like the one I have just described could cause death or serious injury due to a severly weakened structural member. Don't do it. After reading this book you will be able to do the job properly with steel!

Here are the steps to follow when using

plastic filler properly, after a repair has been completed:

1) Sand off the area to be filled. Get rid of all the paint. Use a rough sanding disc if you have a power sander, angle grinder or electric drill. Finish off with a rotating wire brush to get the last scraps of paint out of the deepest part of the dent. If you are doing the job by hand, get the paint off then roughen the area with a sharp screwdriver or a coarse file.

2) Make any last-minute adjustments to the dent.

3) Get the plastic filler out. I use David's P38 Isopon which is widely available in the UK and very reliable for dents and scratches.

4) Follow the makers' instructions to mix the filler. There are two ingredients, the filler and the hardener (the hardener is chemically known as the catalyst).

5) Mix them in quantities that can be used up in a few minutes. You don't want mountains of the stuff going hard while you fiddle about with one little dent!

6) Mix the ingredients on a plastic plate or other plastic surface, because the filler will not stick to it when it hardens. Mix according to the makers' instructions. It is easy to knock off any un-used filler from the plastic surface when you have finished the job.

7) Spread the filler into the dent with a plastic spreader. Normally you get a spreader in the tin when you buy the filler. If the dent is very deep, be prepared to put in two, or even three layers of filler — allowing the first layer to harden before applying the next. A wide spreader will bridge the dent and give you a good guide as to how much filler is needed.

8) Filler hardens (or 'cures') quicker if an excess of hardener is used, or if the air temperature is high. In cold weather the filler will take much longer to harden. Only experience will help you here.

9) Repeat the above steps until the dent is filled, with perhaps a little layer of filler too much.

10) Just before the filler hardens completely, try to shape it with a file such as the special Stanley Surform range of files. These are like cheese graters, and the body filler should come off in strands just like grated cheese. If it has not set it will come away in gooey lumps. It should be just like soft rubber when ready to be shaped. If you leave it till it has hardened fully, it will be much more difficult to shape.

11) Use the file in diagonal strokes to remove as much filler as possible. On curved sections use a rubber sanding block with a suitable grade of wet and dry paper. Smooth off the area until it blends into the

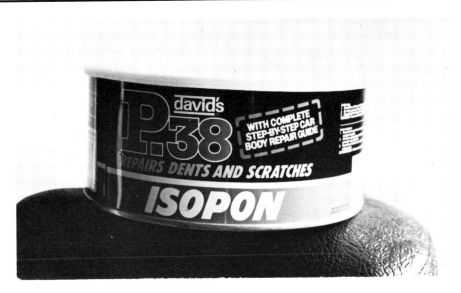

David's P38 Isopon is an ideal plastic filler for use on dents and scratches. There is a full instruction sheet included with every tub.

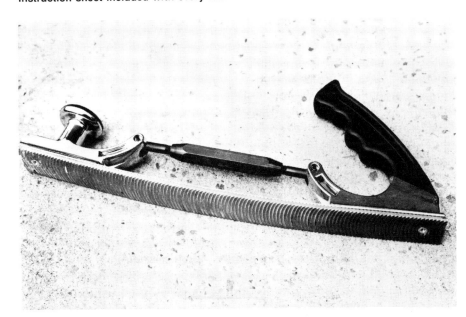

This bodyfile is ideal for smoothing plastic filler. The blade can be adjusted to suit the contours of the panel being worked on. This is a Sykes-Pickavant item.

un-filled area. A proper blend can hardly be seen and is often known as 'featheredging'. The better you get this bit right, the better the final paint job. Don't think paint will hide a shoddy sanding job. The reverse is true. The line of the filler repair will shine through like a beacon if not finished properly.

If you sand off too much, make up another small batch of filler and fill in the mistakes. Keep going till you get it perfect for the reasons mentioned above.

When the filler is dried out properly and sanded to its final contours, spray on a thin coat of primer. This will show up any remaining flaws. These flaws can be filled with 'Spot Putty' which comes in tubes or small tubs. You just smooth it on with a plastic spreader or rubber squeegee in very thin coats. Spot Putty is like a very thick primer, so it takes a little time to dry out. If you find you need a lot of spot putty, then you have made a mistake and should have used more filler. Go back and sort out the problem.

After the spot putty stage, spray on another coat of primer. The job is now ready for painting.

The traditional way of filling dents was with lead. So let's have a look at that technique.

Lead Loading

Just to be sure we know what we are discussing here, lead loading is also known as 'body solder' and 'wiping metal'. These names all refer to the same thing in different countries.

Lead is the old, traditional method of finishing car bodies, while plastic filler is new to the game. Unfortunately the art of lead loading has died out to a large extent as everyone reaches for the quick, easy, no skill needed, plastic filler. We'll have a brief look at lead loading, then you can decide if you want to try it out.

Lead used in lead loading is a mixture of lead and tin. The proportions are 70% lead and 30% tin. This sort of lead has a melting point of about 500 degrees F. Remember these proportions, as you may be tempted to use other types of solder, such as plumbers' solder which may have different proportions. The type of lead you need is frequently advertised in the motoring magazines or you could get it from specialist motor factors.

To lead load you need the following:

1) Sticks of lead as described above,

2) A wooden paddle to apply the lead,

3) A source of heat such as a plumbers' blowlamp,

4) Flux.

These items will be described as we go on.

The lead is applied in this order of events; cleaning, tinning, application, shaping and finishing.

The first job to do is mark out which area is to be loaded. This will depend a lot on the job and the size of the repair. Remove all paint and primer from the area to be filled, plus a little all round as the lead must be blended into the surrounding metal. Use a wire brush or scraper, and if necessary use the blowlamp to burn off the paint. Don't use so much heat you cause distortion in the panel.

A final rub over with some coarse emery paper will help to get a clean, shiny, rust-free surface.

Next, the tinning process. This is the key to working with lead, as the better the tinning process the better the finished job. Once again, use the proper flux for the job, not something borrowed from another trade. Tinning flux contains chemicals which clean the surface being tinned. Apply a little heat to the area being tinned, then apply the liquid flux with a small paint brush.

When the area to be filled, plus a few inches of the surrounding area, has been tinned, you are ready to apply heat and solder.

Using the plumbers' blowlamp, apply a gentle heat to the repair area. A good spread of heat is required, which is one reason that the oxy-acetylene torch is not really suitable, since it tends to be a very

I took this shot at night to try and emphasise the white areas which have been worked on with plastic filler. Some more attention is needed on the left-hand headlamp area.

localised heat source. Heat the steel until it is hot enough to melt the lead stick held against it. This is where the skill comes in, knowing how hot to make the steel.

When the lead is hot enough, a small amount is twisted so that it comes away from the stick of lead. If you have got things under control, you should have a small lump of lead sticking to the metal. Repeat this process until you have several lumps of solder stuck to the tinned area.

Now, using the wooden paddle, or a plumbers' moleskin, heat the lead gently until it starts to melt and look shiny. When you get the temperature right, apply the paddle (which should be soaked in fresh oil to stop it sticking to the lead) or the moleskin to the melted lead and spread it out over the tinned area.

Repeat this process until the tinned area is covered with lead. You may find it very difficult to melt two adjacent lots of lead together, and also difficult to add more lead on top of lead already applied. Don't think you can learn this technique overnight. You can't.

Once the lead is applied and cooled, file it with a body file, but be sure to wear a protective mask, as lead can be a danger to health. Don't ever use a power sander or grinder on lead, because the action is too severe and you will find the lead flying off in little pieces. As well as upsetting your restoration efforts, lead dust is a major health hazard.

You may find you have to fill in little depressions with plastic filler or spot putty, so don't be discouraged if you find you have to do this. It means you were very close to getting it right. Not everyone can master this skill.

The problem is keeping the lead at the correct temperature. Too hot and it will melt completely and drip away. Too cold and it cannot be spread. Beginners to this technique should always start working on a horizontal surface, for working on a vertical surface will just put all your lead on the floor. Leading is a useful technique, but one which needs a lot of practice to get right.

If you are in any doubt about your ability to use lead, then don't. Plastic filler if used properly is much easier to use and still gives a professional finish. The secret is putting enough effort into it!

Now that we have either used lead or plastic and have a smooth, clean body, we need to have a closer look at paint.

Paint

What is paint? Paint is a protective coating applied to cars to prevent steel rusting. Obvious? Well, yes it is in a way, but it is surprising how often people only think of paint as a decoration. Professional painters can now get ready to throw their hands in the air in horror as I over-simplify a difficult subject.

Paint actually consists of several parts, the

main parts being solvents, pigments and binders. As I said earlier, I don't want to go into the subject of paint too deeply, but a few words on these main ingredients may give you a better understanding of the subject. Whole books have been written just about paint, so I have considerably simplified the subject in these notes!

The solvent is the agent which allows the paint to be spread over the surface being painted. If you did not have the solvent you would have a lump of pigment and binder. The solvent actually evaporates when the paint is applied, its only job being to aid the spreading or carrying process. So, when you spray paint you need more solvent (or thinners) than if you were brushing the paint on. The spray paint has to be diluted in order to be sprayed.

The binder is the agent which causes the paint to 'stick' or adhere to the surface being painted. The binder holds the particles of pigment together to form a coat, or thickness, of the paint.

The pigment is the colour of the paint. Pigments vary enormously in type and source. Some are man-made, others occur naturally. Many types of paint cannot be mixed, so an old vehicle with a certain type of paint may not be suitable to re-paint with another type of paint.

I hope this quick outline description of paint will help your painting efforts!

Why do we need paint? The answer is simple; it decorates and it protects. In this Chapter the emphasis is on protection rather than decoration, so if you want more information about paints and painting, I suggest you have a look in the Bibliography section at the end of the book.

In order to do the protecting job properly, the surface to be painted must be prepared properly. Normally this involves cleaning the surface (which may involve removing wax polishes etc) and in many cases involves removing old paint. The first recommended action is to steam clean the body, and this is particularly effective on the underside, such as the frame and chassis parts.

The only way to be sure of eliminating the problem of paints not being compatible, is to remove ALL the old paint, and go back to bare metal. This is done with paint removing chemicals, scrapers, grinders, and rotating wire brushes. Make no mistake, it is a long, dirty, unpleasant business. It must be done completely to be fully effective.

When all the old paint is removed, make any repairs which may come to light as a result of the paint removal. It is surprising how much is hidden by paint! Any old plastic filler repairs may need to be renewed.

This dealer has a wide selection of new and second-hand spares for the Cortina, Anglia and Corsair. As the ad says, just phone and ask!

BRUSH OR SPRAY?

Having got all the old paint off, you now need to decide; brush or spray. To many of you the choice seems obvious – spray. However it is worth remembering that a good brush painted job will stand up to quite close scrutiny and may well be all you need for a 'drive-to-work' car. There are a number of brush on paints available, and I suggest you enquire at your local motor factor, or read the monthly magazines.

The majority will want to have their vehicle spray painted, as almost everyone knows someone who can spray. At least, it seems that way until you have a look at their work. Paint sprayed over tyres, windscreen rubbers, chromework and so on. Poor preparation is reflected in a low price. You get what you pay for. Having spent a long time working on a car, don't you think it is worth having the best possible paint job you can afford?

PROTECTIVE PAINTS

I have used two very different protective paints on my cars. These are Comma Stoprust and Finnigan's Hammerite. Let's have a look at these two, see how they differ and give you some idea about what to look for in other protective paints.

COMMA STOPRUST

This red-coloured paint is available from many sources, but Halfords seem to keep a regular supply in the UK.

The product guarantees protection against

corrosion and also provides a primer. It contains no lead and conforms to European regulations on lead poisoning. Other advantages include the ability to withstand temperatures up to 300 degrees C, making it useful for exhaust systems.

Oil, grease, chemicals, loose paint and rust must be removed prior to application, and it is recommended that only firmly adherent rust should remain. The area to be painted should also be treated with cellulose thinners.

As with similar products, a very comprehensive instruction sheet is packed with every tin, and for best results you must take a few minutes to read the instructions.

Finnigan's Hammerite

This special paint air dries in just 15 minutes and provides an enamel-type finish which repels dirt and water like a non-stick pan. Again there is a full data sheet available with the product, but the basic guidelines are; the surface must be bone dry, and all loose rust and scale must be removed.

Apply one heavy coat quickly (a minimum thickness of four thousandths of an inch is recommended), then remove any surplus paint by going over the job again with a brush. If more than one coat is needed, the second coat should be applied as soon as the first one is dry — which should be about 15 minutes.

Hammerite is fairly well known and is available in a selection of colours. It is probably the best paint available for chassis protection. I have seen a few jobs finished in Hammerite that were so clean and shiny you could eat your dinner off them!

Aerosols

I have never been very successful with aerosol painting, but plenty of people seem to use them successfully, so I must have been doing something wrong.

Make sure you have the correct colour before spraying. Remember that your original paint colour may have faded over the years, so a coat of new paint from the aerosol may not match too well.

Follow the instructions on the can, and keep shaking the can to mix the paint. Keep the can upright and make a few practise passes before pressing the button. Generally, you need to keep the can about 8 inches from the panel.

Spray several thin coats, leaving suitable time to dry between applications. If you need to spray horizontal panels, hold the can at about 45 degrees to the surface and spray from above.

Remember, as with all spraying, if you do

Comma Stoprust has a five year guarantee and will stabilise rust as well as prime. It is available in several sizes and is ideal for chassis painting and priming.

I picked this spraygun up at an autojumble for just £1 — and it worked too! The flexible adapter can be bent to any shape (within reason) and is ideal for getting into chassis box sections.

not prepare the job properly you will get paint on tyres, chrome trim and glass. Take care for best results.

Underseal

There are several types of underseal available, but they all claim to protect against corrosion. Some are heavy enough to offer protection against 'drumming' caused by body panels vibrating. This can cause a car to be very unpleasant to drive at certain speeds.

The basic requirements before undersealing is done is to remove all loose rust, dirt and grease. A good heavy coating is best, and if required you can add other coats later. The underseal usually goes on very shiny, but as it dries out it becomes more of a matt finish.

I frequently use underseal on the front and rear panels, especially under the bumper which needs a bit of extra protection. Underseal is also helpful on sills, but some people won't use it there if the sill should be painted the same colour as the car. It depends on what you want. Underseal is so widely used on sills that I cannot see a great problem. Remember NOT to block vital drain holes in the bottom of the sill.

If you get underseal on a surface where you don't want it – such as a door panel or on glass, it can usually be wiped off with a rag soaked in white spirit or paraffin. Read the manufacturer's instructions on the tin.

Leaking Windscreen?

A leaking windscreen could be the root cause of all that bodywork you have had to do. If water gets in and accumulates on the floor, it will not be very long before you are patching the floor and replacing chassis members. Comma Seek'n Seal is a low viscosity windscreen sealant which flows into minute holes and cracks in rubber. Within hours Seak'n Seal is absorbed by the rubber to form a new flexible seal. However, being a liquid it will not fill large holes in rubber surrounds. You will need a new windscreen surround for that job.

The surface to be repaired must be clean and dry, and time must be allowed between coats. After an hour remove any excess with white spirits.

There are many other windscreen sealing products, and I have also used a tube of black sealer material which proved very effective but needed a lot of wiping up, as it proved to be rather messy in my hands! I have not seen this particular material on sale recently, but a browse through the accessory shops will provide you with several similar options.

T-Cut

I can do no better than repeat what it says on the T-Cut tin, 'Gives showroom appearance to discoloured paintwork' and 'Removes oxidation, road film, tar spots from paintwork.

T-Cut is a liquid which you apply with a soft cloth. You work just a small area at a time and it will clean any type of paintwork – even paint which has never had

This little plant spray cost just 90 pence in the local hardware shop. It is ideal for spraying into tight corners and into chassis box sections.

any attention for years.

After working an area, wipe it off with a clean dry cloth. The results can be amazing, depending on the paint problem and how bad it was. Another advantage is that paint can be touched up without any further preparation after using T-Cut.

It is available from most motor factors and Halfords usually have it in the UK.

Colour Codes

If you need to buy paint to have your car re-sprayed, how do you know what colour the paint is? Yes, I know it is red, or blue or white, but there could be dozens of different reds, blues and so on. The vehicle manufacturer has helped you here, but you may not know it!

T-Cut is great for restoring dull or mistreated paintwork. It needs a bit of arm-work though, and for the best results treat a small area at a time.

Somewhere on your car, (it may be on the top of the inner wing, under the hood) is a metal plate which has a lot of numbers and letters. One or two of these code letters is the paint code. For example, if you go to the paint supplier and ask for Ford colour BH there is a fair chance you will get Caribbean Turquoise. They may need to ask you a few questions about year of manufacturer and so on, but it works! They'll go away and mix you a tin of the correct shade.

I suggest you have a look for the Vehicle Identification Plate on your car.

Chassis Protection

Once you have finished all the bodywork and the chassis repairs, and applied paint, it time to think about preserving the box sections of the chassis. One way to do this is to buy the Waxoyl kit available from many car supermarkets and motor factors. This consists of a waxy protective substance which is sprayed into all the nooks and crannies, providing protection against

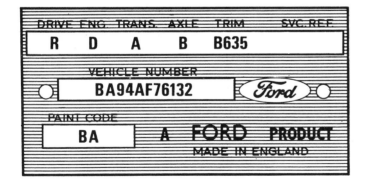

This is a Ford Identification Plate which is fixed to the right hand mudguard apron, inside the engine compartment. BA is the paint code, which in this case means Ermine White. (Courtesy Ford Motor Company).

127

rust. A special spray injector is available which forces the Waxoyl into every corner. If applied correctly, there should be very few areas of a car which are not protected.

Waxoyl can be over-painted, although you will have to wait at least 48 hours to allow it to penetrate. The last time I looked, there was a very comprehensive instruction sheet supplied with Waxoyl, and if you want the best results, you should follow it carefully.

Waxoyl is probably the best solution available, although it could be a little expensive for some pockets. Try the following cheap alternative.

Cheap Spraygun

To get into box sections and inside 'top hat' you need a thin tube and some sort of pump, to spray the protecting fluid – whatever it is. One cheap pump is the little plant spray sold in garden shops. I bought one for just 90 pence.

You can use it as it is, or modify it as follows. Remove the spray nozzle, and fit a length of plastic pipe. You can use the type of plastic used for windscreen washers, which is also the same as the plastic pipe used in aquarium shops to pump air into fish tanks. Alternatively, you can use a larger diameter plastic pipe which is available in 'home brew' shops to syphon beer and wine. Whichever pipe you use, you need about four feet of it, so that you can get right into the sills from either end.

Fix one end of your plastic pipe to the spray. Use glue or Araldite for this and

Comma Seek'n'Seal is ideal for sealing leaking windscreen rubbers. It will seal small holes and being a liquid will flow into the holes easily.

give it plenty of time to dry. The other end of the pipe needs to be blocked off completely. You could fold over the end, clip it with a staple to be sure, then fill in the end with more Araldite. Alternatively, screw a self-tapping screw into the pipe to seal it off. Glue it to keep it in position. Now, with a pin, make three or four holes about

an inch from the blocked off end of the pipe.

The best way to test this is to place the pipe in a plastic bottle such as a Coca-Cola bottle and operate the pump. Use paraffin and fresh engine oil for the tests. You want a nice steady flow from the holes and enough to give an all round coverage to the insides of the bottle. Experiment with the holes until you get it right and with the ratio of paraffin and oil.

Now apply the same mixture to the box sections of your car. The paraffin acts as a carrier for the oil and will evaporate quite quickly, leaving the oily layer on all the insides of the box sections. This cheap method could save you a fortune in rebuilding the chassis.

You might have to repeat the process every year, but it is a cheap and useful method of preventing rust starting on the inside of box sections.

In the previous Chapters I have attempted to show you how to work sheet metal from basic principles, through to much more complicated restoration techniques. To illustrate many of the techniques the next Chapter is the Cortina Restoration feature.

I hope you found something interesting in Panel Craft. Good luck with your future restorations!

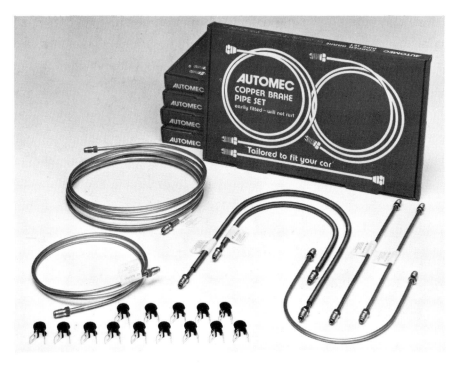

Nothing to do with body panels, but I thought you ought to know about copper brake pipes which will not rust. Contact Automec Equipment & Parts, Arden House, West Street, Leighton Buzzard, Bedfordshire LU7 7DD, England.

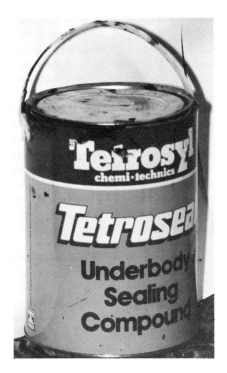

Underseal comes in several types, but this type can be brushed on easily. It protects and can also be used to prevent panels from noise caused by drumming.

OLD FORD SPARES SERVICE

Estate rear floor NEW PANEL £25	Steel front wings NEW GENUINE FORD £200 pr
Front wheel brg kits NEW £9.25	Fuel pumps NEW £14
Used doors Excellent No rust £15	Bonnets & Boot lids Excellent Used £12
Front screen rubbers Excellent used £8	Headlamp bezels Used As New £8 pr
Engine mounts NEW £6	Front exhaust section GT £16
Quarter bumpers Very good used £10 pr	Rear screen rubbers Excellent used £8

PRICES DO NOT INCLUDE POSTAGE & PACKING.
PLEASE RING TO CONFIRM CARRIAGE CHARGES.
WEEKDAY EVENINGS AFTER 5.30
OR ANYTIME AT THE WEEKEND.

Rugby (0788) 816286

This dealer has a variety of new and second hand spares available for Cortina, Anglia, Capri/Classic and several other Fords from 1951 onwards.

This is the sort of job which is ideal for plastic filler. You can see where the old filler has been removed during work on the panel (just above the hole). When filled and smoothed down again it will be an invisible repair.

Cortina Restoration

The Cortina enthusiast's ultimate ambition (well, mine anyway!) – to own a Lotus Cortina. These two splendid examples of the marque were pictured at Cheltenham in 1986.

About the Club

The club was founded in the Summer of 1982, having seen that there was a need for people to band together to buy spares and help preserve a much loved vehicle.

Twenty-five founder members quickly helped to 'seed' the Club's formation with initially just two officials – Roger Raisey, who became the membership Secretary and Mike Pratt who produced the newsletter. However, it became obvious that help was needed and the club now boasts two Spares Secretaries (Colin Seaward in Kent and Steve Ollier in Lancashire) and an Events Secretary (Dave Dance in Oxfordshire).

The Club now has regular meetings in Lancashire, Nottinghamshire, Avon, Kent, Essex and the Midlands once a month, and furthermore the Club holds its own weekend event – the National A.G.M. during the Summer at a delightful place named Hagley Hall near Stourbridge, West Midlands. This annual event is now well enough known by other invited Ford related Clubs to warrant the simple statement, 'See you at Hagley.'

Naturally spares form a large chunk of club activity and the club is always sourc-

ing these elusive bits, and has been able to buy obsolete stock from Fords. The Club has recently negotiated the re-manufactured of front wings. The Newsletter gives members the opportunity to sell their unwanted items, and to see who, outside the club has items needed by members.

Advertising on a monthly basis in a national magazine helps considerably towards promoting the club and in this way non-members and the Trade can let us know what they can offer the club and we also find new members – all helping to keep the club going.

The club are presently some 700-strong and look forward to strengthening their ties within the Classic Car Movement in the hope of perpetuating the memories of a much-loved and well sold car (one and a quarter million cars in four years) which in rallying guise dominated the world at the time.

M.T. Pratt,
Club Chairman,
64 Monckton Drive,
Townville,
nr Castleford,
W Yorkshire.

INTRODUCTION

The following pages contain a detailed photo-spread of Ford Cortina MKI bodyshells undergoing repairs and major restoration. I didn't have enough photographs of my own cars, so you will see about half a dozen different bodyshells involved. In this way I have produced a comprehensive illustration of all the possible jobs you will come across. To help you identify all the body parts, Ford Motor Company have allowed me to use illustrations from the official Cortina Parts List.

Captions describe what is being done in each photograph.

Almost everything shown in these pages has been described in the rest of the book. Some of what you see may well be beyond your capabilities. Don't worry. Everyone has to start somewhere, so if you are keen, try something quite simple to start with. As your confidence grows you will be able to tackle bigger and more complicated jobs. Don't forget to join the Club!

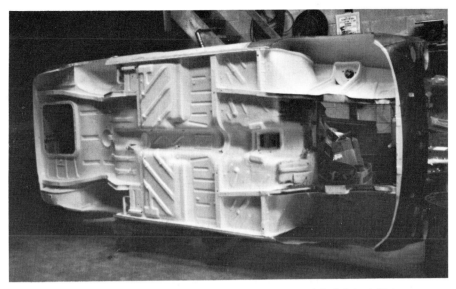

What every restored bodyshell should look like when the work is finished. Not everyone has the facilities or experience to tackle a complete restoration, but anyone can tackle small repair jobs to start gaining experience. Once started, bodywork and restoration will provide much greater satisfaction than almost any mechanical work. (Photo by A.G. Coates of Classic Components.)

An early, 'round side-light' two-door bodyshell undergoing restoration. Work done to a high standard, and properly protected, should last another 25 years. (Photo by A.G.Coates of Classic Components.)

TA

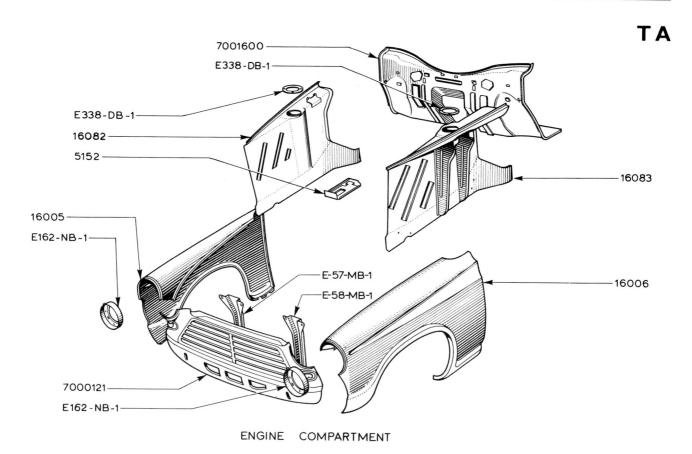

7001600
E338-DB-1
E338-DB-1
16082
5152
16005
E162-NB-1
E-57-MB-1
E-58-MB-1
7000121
E162-NB-1
16083
16006

ENGINE COMPARTMENT

The main body panels comprising the engine compartment. The illustration is from the official Ford Cortina Parts List. (Courtesy Ford Motor Company.)

This front corner is showing serious signs of rust after 21 years. Most of the damage is on the front panel; the wing is relatively sound. The car cost the author £25, so a lot of work was anticipated. Details of the repairs to this section continue on the following pages.

Compare this front panel and inner wing assembly with the Parts List drawing. The drivers' side front wing is seen clamped to the front panel prior to welding. It is vital that all the panels are correctly located before welding is attempted. (Photo by Roger Raisey.)

The entire front assembly, including inner and outer wings and front panel, has been replaced on this bodyshell. The large jig ensures that all the major panels are correctly located. A job like this could be tackled in the home workshop, but you need to be sure you know what you are doing! (Photo by A.G.Coates of Classic Components.)

New front panel, wings and headlamp rings have been welded on this later bodyshell. Most of the bodywork is now finished on the front of this car, and some of the mechanical assemblies can now be fitted. (Photo by Roger Raisey.)

Part of the rusty section cut out of the front panel. Another vertical cut has to be made to remove about an inch of the front panel, where the rust hole is. Once this section is replaced, the rust under the chrome grill will be tackled.

The welding is finished and the surface has been cleaned up with the angle grinder. Compare this with the above photo!

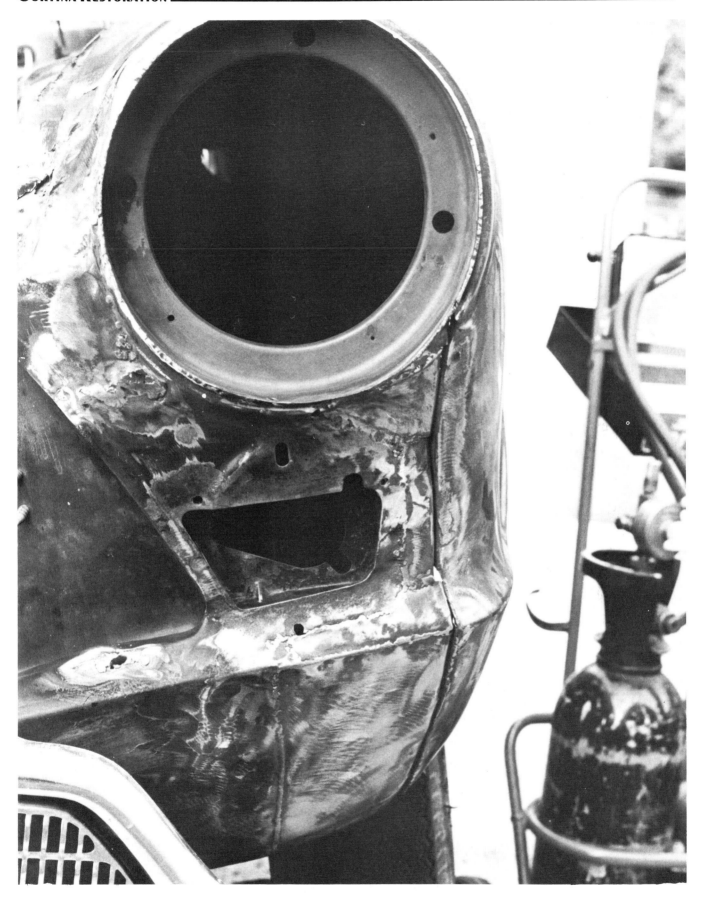

The full view of that repaired front panel — including my mistake! The two big holes in the headlamp ring should be horizontal, and not at an angle as shown. I had to re-drill the holes. The reason is the car was up on ONE ramp for a long time and I forgot when lining up. Don't repeat my mistake!

WARNING

Welding under the wing can be dangerous unless precautions are taken. Remove all underseal from the welding area to prevent fumes. Check what is on the 'other' side of the panel to be welded. Ensure that all previous glass fibre 'repairs' have been removed, otherwise they could ignite, giving off dangerous fumes. Have a fire extinguisher handy before welding. A squeezy bottle of water is better than nothing, and could save a serious fire. Keep the flame away from electrical wiring. Ensure that the car is safely supported on axle stands or ramps before working under a wing. NEVER work on a car supported by just a jack.

Having repaired the other side as described in the photos, I next tackled the driver's side front panel, which had suffered similar damage. On this side I had to replace the wing as well, but it only cost me £10 from a scrap yard.

A home made patch for the front chassis leg. You can buy custom made patches, but this one is quite simple to make. Remember to use a template.

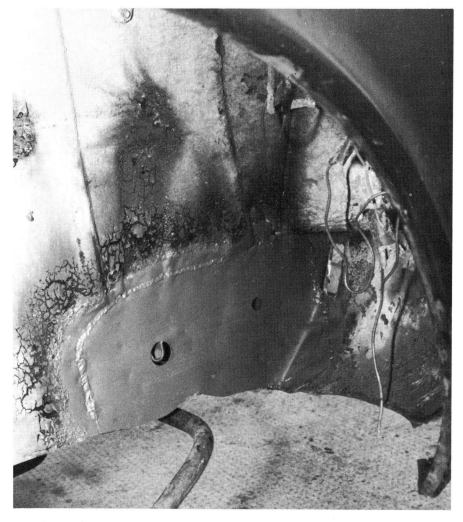

The repair patch for the front chassis welded in place. After a few coats of protective paint, and some underseal you will never know it has been repaired. The large hole in the patch allows me to insert a plastic tube to inject rust inhibitor.

All front end work is completed and the car has been painted with primer. Next stop is the paint shop. You have to decide how much time and effort is justified for your car — and the use to which it will be put. Drive-to-work cars probably get less attention than show cars! (Photo by Roger Raisey.)

Don't create metalwork which leaves you ashamed to open the bonnet! The ex-Roger Clark rally car again, just to let you see the standard you should be aiming for in your restoration work. The whole car is shown in the Introduction to the book.

Two ways to tackle the same job. On this car, a home made patch has been fabricated and welded into position. This is a common area for Cortinas to rust so LMC Panels produced the patch shown below. (Photo by Roger Raisey.)

The LMC patch clamped in position prior to welding. I had a little more corrosion than usual in this area, so I will need to insert another patch above the bought panel. The welding clamps shown allow you to clamp and put tack welds in between the jaws. This can be very useful sometimes.

Although this inner wing looks frightening, don't let it put you off. I mentally split the panel into four areas and patched each in turn. The main problem area is in the centre, just below and to the left of the hole. In a later photograph you can see the full extent of the damage. Cut a bit out, weld and go on to the next area, that's the secret.

TB

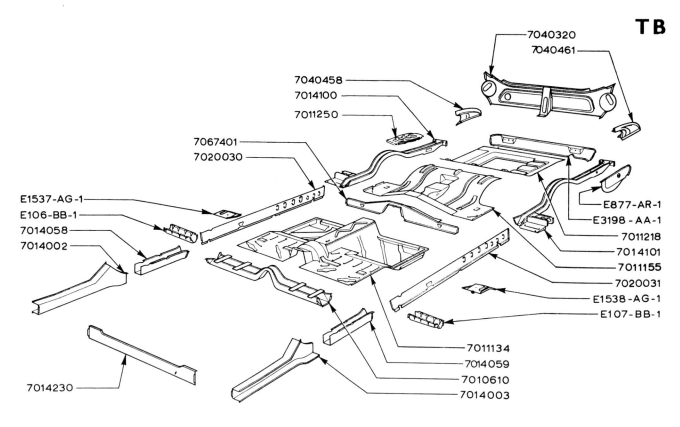

FLOOR AND MEMBERS

The floor and main chassis members, taken from the Cortina Parts List again. Drawings like these are very helpful to restorers, as they give you a good idea what to expect before you crawl underneath the car. (Courtesy Ford Motor Company.)

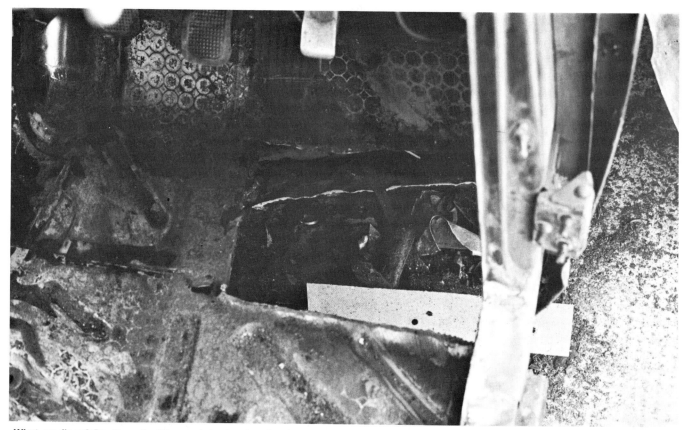

What, no floor? Don't panic, this repair took only a few hours and cost about £10 to £15. You'll need some sheet steel to form a floor section, and a front outrigger/jacking point. Once again, do a bit at a time, and don't let the job get to you!

Cortina Mk 1
1962–66

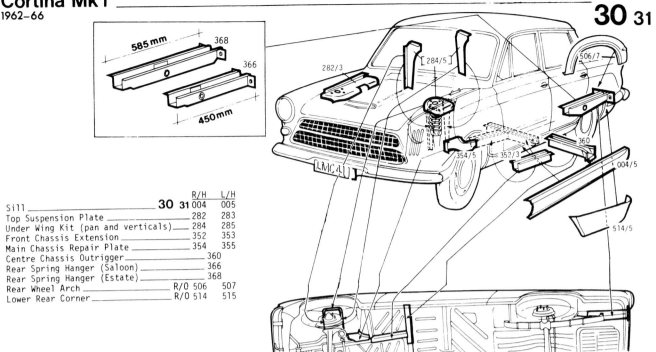

	R/H	L/H
Sill _____ **30** 31	004	005
Top Suspension Plate _____	282	283
Under Wing Kit (pan and verticals) ___	284	285
Front Chassis Extension _____	352	353
Main Chassis Repair Plate _____	354	355
Centre Chassis Outrigger _____		360
Rear Spring Hanger (Saloon) _____		366
Rear Spring Hanger (Estate) _____		368
Rear Wheel Arch _____ R/O	506	507
Lower Rear Corner _____ R/O	514	515

What would I do without LMC Panels? I have used their panels for a number of years and they really are good. Order through a distributor or see the address in the Address section later in the book.

The fragile part of the inner wing. You can see the pencilled outline where I am going to cut to remove the rust. You have to be very careful doing this sort of repair, due to possible fire problems. Ensure that all underseal, underfelt, wiring, radio aerial cables etc. have been removed BEFORE welding. On some cars the voltage regulator is mounted on the inside of the passenger-side inner wing, next to the glove box. This must be removed before lighting the torch. It just isn't worth the hassle having a fire.

This general view shows a number of problem areas. The outer sill is removed and the inner sill is being repaired. The front of the inner sill, where it meets the inner wing has had some work done, while the weld outline of a new front chassis outrigger can be seen at the bottom of the inner wing.

A new piece of steel clamped in place to form the bottom of the inner wing and inner sill. I am using two Inter-grip welding clamps and a Mole clamp to hold the repair panels. Note that I have NOT cut all the rust away, as I will use what's left to get the correct shape for the repair patch. Without the clamps the A Post will move about.

The bottom of the inner wing and inner sill in close-up. The outer sill is shown clamped in position and is being lined up with the door. The remaining rust on the lower part of the inner wing will be cut off and welded to the fresh steel.

On the other side of the car, I chose to break the spot welds holding the wing to the inner sill. Using the piece of steel shown, I wedged the wing away from the inner wing to gain access to the front of the sill. You can see where I formed new repair sections at the bottom of the A Post. This type of work is time-consuming, but pays off in the long term. This type of restoration is noticed, so try and get it right!

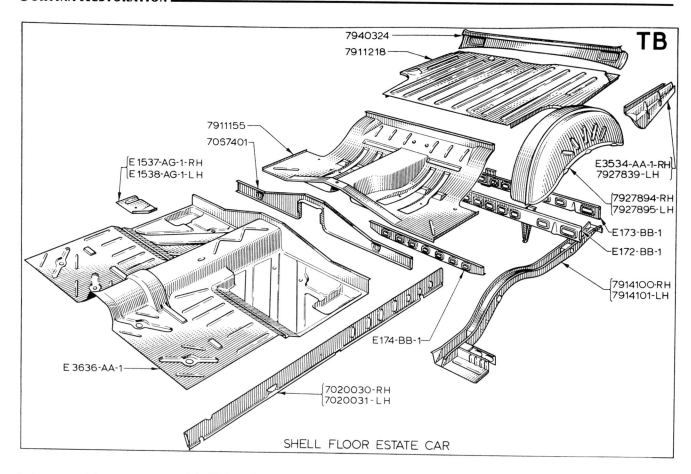

Just so you estate car owners won't feel left out (and for completeness) I've included the estate car floor panel drawing from the Parts List. (Courtesy Ford Motor Company.)

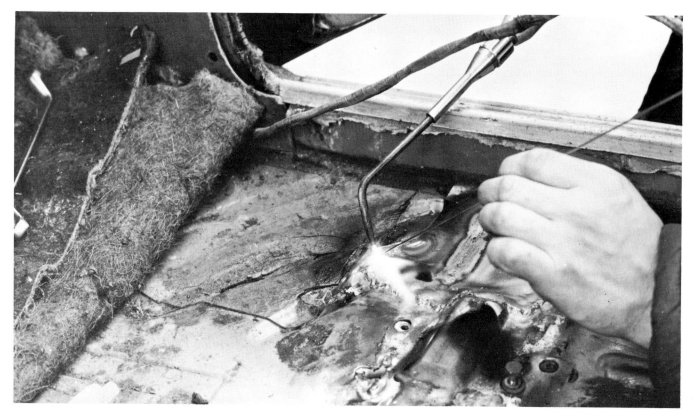

Patching the floor near the seat mounting holes. I've made up a repair patch from a piece of steel and am welding it into position. I'll have to go underneath and complete the welding, as there is a chassis outrigger underneath which MUST be welded to the floor. Note the wiring loom held up out of the way, tied to the steering wheel with a bit of scrap wire. Better than a burnt loom!

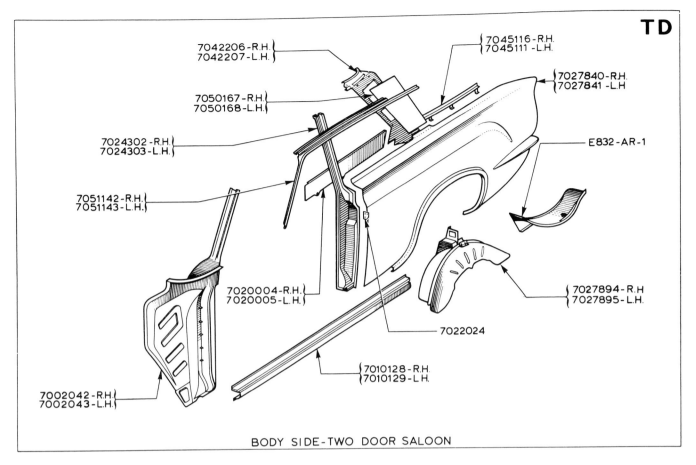

TD

7042206-R.H.
7042207-L.H.

7045116-R.H.
7045111-L.H.

7027840-R.H.
7027841-L.H

7050167-R.H.
7050168-L.H.

E832-AR-1

7024302-R.H.
7024303-L.H.

7051142-R.H.
7051143-L.H.

7020004-R.H.
7020005-L.H.

7027894-R.H
7027895-L.H.

7022024

7002042-R.H.
7002043-L.H.

7010128-R.H.
7010129-L.H.

BODY SIDE-TWO DOOR SALOON

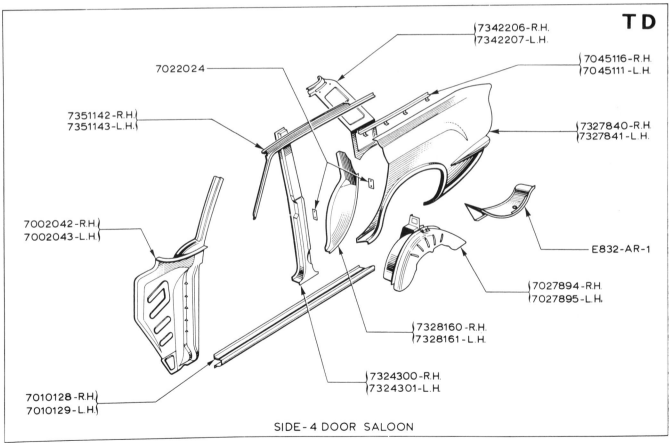

TD

7342206-R.H.
7342207-L.H.

7045116-R.H.
7045111-L.H.

7022024

7351142-R.H.
7351143-L.H.

7327840-R.H.
7327841-L.H.

7002042-R.H.
7002043-L.H.

E832-AR-1

7027894-R.H.
7027895-L.H.

7328160-R.H.
7328161-L.H.

7324300-R.H.
7324301-L.H.

7010128-R.H.
7010129-L.H.

SIDE-4 DOOR SALOON

The side panel drawings for both the two- and four-door saloons. Some of these panels are the same on both cars, and several re-manufactured panels are available. (Courtesy Ford Motor Company.)

This is a modification I have used on two Cortinas now. Initially, I could not get front outriggers, so I adapted rear spring hanger panels. You can see where I welded on a square washer to re-inforce the jacking point. The steel tube assembly built into the panel (normally used to locate the rear spring) provides masses of strength. I reckon it is pretty neat! You can buy the front outrigger from Classic Components.

BELOW. Moving back along the car now, the new sills are clamped in position prior to welding. Great care is necessary to get the optimum fit. That door looks like it will need some attention! (Photo by Roger Raisey.)

'Ere, where does this go then? The author examines a rear chassis section as he assembles all the parts needed to revive 'HTB'. The MKI Cortina Owner's Club are having new front wings re-manufactured. Glass fibre front wings are available, but you know what I think about them!

Rear wheel arch rot. This example is probably worse than most, but it can be corrected by fitting a new repair panel. Great care is needed if you choose to weld this repair panel, as distortion can be a serious problem here. You can also see where the end of the inner sill has had new steel welded in.

The new outer sill clamped in position, and you can see what is missing from the rear wheel arch! I have marked a cutting line on the rear quarter panel to show where the new wheel arch goes. Before I do that, I will complete work on the sill. (Inset) This plate carries the seat-belt mounting, and I have added a few re-inforcing welds because the plate was not properly fixed to the inner sill.

TD

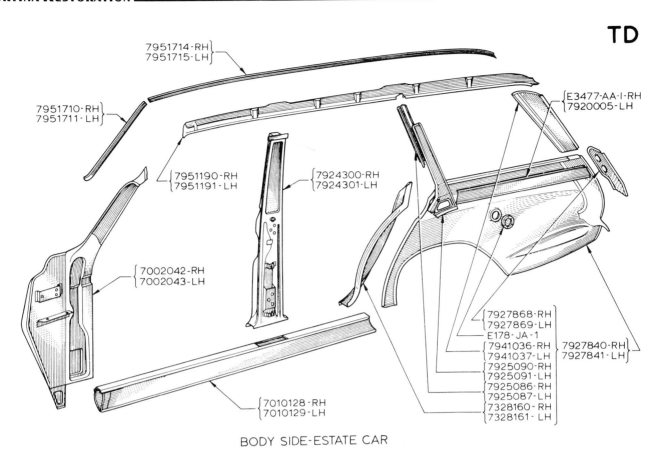

BODY SIDE-ESTATE CAR

The estate car body side drawings from the Parts List. (Courtesy Ford Motor Company.)

The cutting line on the rear quarter panel, ready for the tin snips. The rot on the wheel arch lip is typical of a car this age. Remember that what you see will actually be worse when you cut out this section. The inner wheel arch will undoubtedly be much worse!

And as predicted it is MUCH worse. All this rusty steel will have to be repaired before the outer repair panel can be fitted. Use small patch panels with plenty of 'V's to make the inner arch repair sections.

(Left) The wheel arch repair panel clamped in place. I chose to seam weld this section with the oxy-acetylene torch. This might have been a mistake, as some distortion of the quarter panel was inevitable. (Right) The repair panel welded at the front, where it meets the C Post. This required some special attention to make sure the door would open and shut correctly.

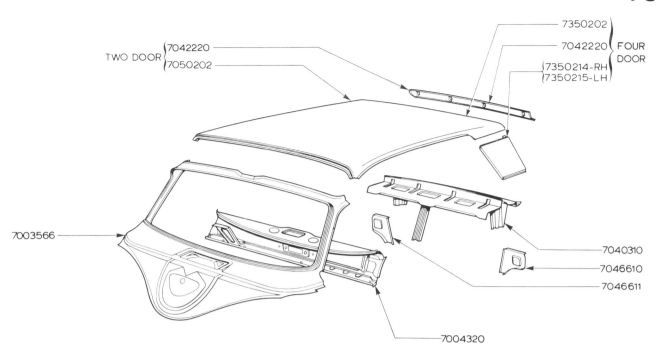

ROOF, WINDSCREEN OPENING PANEL & REAR PACKAGE TRAY

To complete the body panel drawings, this is the roof and windscreen panels. Rust in the pillars of the windscreen panel is common, but can normally be repaired. I believe these panels would be very hard to find now. (Courtesy Ford Motor Company.)

The wheel arch repair nearing completion. It is not apparent from this photograph, but some distortion of the rear quarter panel had to be dressed with hammer and dolly (a bit difficult due to the inner wheel arch) then filled with plastic filler. This job is more difficult than it looks. Beware!

I made several repair sections for this rear chassis section (it is above the rear axle). Basically it consists of a patch, on top of which is a repaired 'original' strengthening section. At the right you can see the next job — cutting out a previously repaired section. The repair was a typical mechanic's 'stick a lump of scrap steel on top' bodge. Okay, perhaps for a quick MOT, but no good as a restoration attempt. This repair is fully described in the Chapter on Frame and Chassis Repairs.

Looking under the petrol tank, towards the driver's side. The double skin section, behind the spring, is shown here in the 'as-found' condition. I had to repair this in several parts. A new outer corner panel has already been fitted in this shot. This repair is fully described in the Chapter on Floors.

Looking into the spare wheel well from the passenger's side. The new right hand wall of the well has been made up from two pieces of steel and welded into place. The outer corner has already been cut away. This allows better access to the spare wheel well. The repair is fully described in the Chapter on Floors. It is not difficult to do, but gives lots of backache when you lean over the edge of the boot to weld the bottom sections in place!

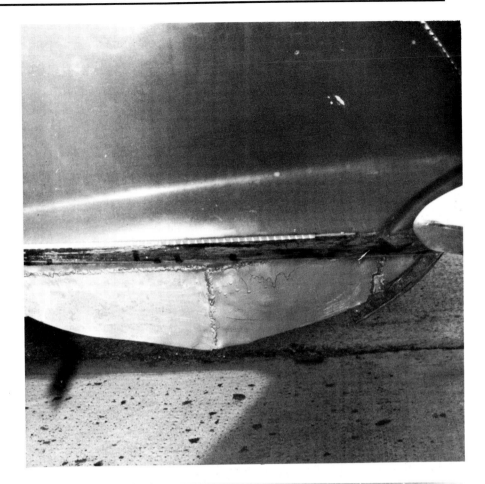

The driver's side rear corner panel, 'as found'. Yet again, this example is probably worse than most, but about what I expected from a £25 car. The second layer of rot is the double skin section which is also shown on the opposite page. The black painted part indicates almost exactly where the new panel will weld on. It can be blended into that styling 'hump' to provide an invisible mend!

Back to the passenger's side, rear corner again and the repair section clamped in place. You can see where the repair section blends into the styling of the original panel. This is a trial fitting as I have still to fit the lower section of the wheel well repair.

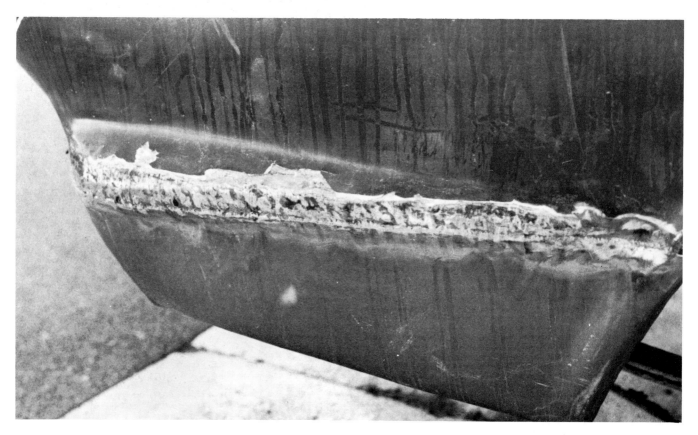

The rear corner repair panel welded in position. Now it needs a few passes with the angle grinder and a little hammer and dolly work. The holes you see were from a previous repair. It was so well done I only found out it was plastic filler when it started to burn during the welding! I'll fill the holes in by 'Blobbing.'

And so, off to the paint shop. If you have followed the advice in this book, you will be able to tackle most of the jobs necess- ary for a complete bodyshell restoration. If something IS beyond your capabilities, don't attempt it. Nothing looks worse than a bodged job. This nicely-restored GT bodyshell will provide years of use for its owner. (Photo by Roger Raisey.)

I have to drive mine to work every day, so it will take me longer to get 'CAN' re- stored. Must fix those doors next.
Next to the hedge is 'HTB' awaiting resto- ration, while my Capri hides under a cover. Perhaps doing one at a time would be a better idea.
There must be an engine in here, some- where...

Useful Addresses

LMC Panels, Quartermaster Road, West Wilts Trading Estate, Westbury, Wiltshire, BA13 4JT.

Manufacturers of high quality replacement body panels and chassis repair sections. Order through distributors, or in case of difficulty, contact them at the above address.

MKI Cortina Owners Club, Membership Secretary, D. Payne, 1 Range Road, Gravesend, Kent. Chairman, M.T. Pratt, 64 Monckton Drive, Townville, Castleford, West Yorkshire.

The club for the MKI Cortina Owner.

MKI Cortina Parts Centre, (Mail Order only) to 18 King Edward Avenue, Hastings, East Sussex, TN34 2NQ.

Suppliers of new and used MKI Cortina, Corsair and Anglia 105E spares.

Classic Components, Ickornshaw Mill, Ickornshaw, Cowling, nr. Keighley, West Yorkshire.

Manufacturer and supplier of MKI Cortina repair panels and other spares.

Russell Motor Services, 8 Walker Wood, Baildon, Shipley, West Yorkshire, BD17 5BE.

Manufacturers and suppliers of Louvring Moulds.

A.T.A. Engineering Processes, Ebberns Road, Hemel Hempstead, Herts, HP3 9QX.

Suppliers of Wedgelock temporary fastening systems and drilling aids.

Gas Control Equipment Ltd, Peel Road, West Pimbo, Skelmersdale, Lancashire, Wn8 9QA.

Manufacturers of gas welding equipment and products.

Old Ford Spares Service, 24 Marlborough Road, Rugby, Warwickshire, CV22 6DD.

Supplier of Ford spares for MKI Cortina, Anglia 105E, Capri/Classic, and many other Fords from 1951 onwards.

Sykes-Pickavant Ltd, Kilnhouse Lane, Lytham St Annes, Lancashire, FY8 3DU.

Manufacturers of automotive and industrial service tools, and Speedline Hand Tools. Order through distributors, or in case of difficulty, contact them at the above address.

Crewkerne Tyre Co., North Street Trading Estate, Crewkerne, Somerset.

Supplier of Lotus Cortina spares.

Bibliography

Osprey's 15-title restoration series, particularly *'How to Restore Sheet Metal Bodywork'* by Bob Smith, and *'How to Restore Chassis and Monocoque Bodywork'* by Tommy Sandham. See also, *'How to Restore Fibreglass Bodywork'* by Miles Wilkins.

Haynes Publishing's *'The Car Bodywork Repair Manual'* by Lindsay Porter.

Haynes Publishing's *'Guide to Purchase & D.I.Y Restoration of the Morris Minor & 1000'*, by Lindsay Porter.

Haynes Publishing's *'Guide to Purchase & D.I.Y Restoration of the Ford Escort and Cortina,* by Kim Henson.

Petersen's *'Basic Bodywork & Painting'*, by Petersen Publishing Company.

Petersen's *'Auto Restoration Tips & Techniques'* by Petersen Publishing Company.

Brooklands Books *'Basic Painting Tips & Techniques'*, compiled from Hot Rod Magazine.

Brooklands Books *'Basic Bodywork Tips & Techniques'*, compiled from Hot Rod Magazine.

HP Books *'Metal Fabricator's Handbook/Race & Custom Car'* by Ron Fournier.

HP Books *'Paint & Body Handbook'* by Don Taylor & Larry Hofer.

Temple Press, *'Thoroughbred & Classic Cars Guide to Bodywork Restoration.'*

Heineman Educational Books, *'The Repair of Vehicle Bodies'* by A. Robinson. (Published on behalf of the Vehicle Builders' and Repairers' Association).

Goodheart-Willcox Company, *'Autobody Repairing and Repainting,'* by Bill Toboldt.

Morris Minor Centre, *'Durable Car Ownership'* by Charles Ware.

Orbis Publishing, *'Panel Beating and Car Restoration'*, by Donald Wait.

Osprey Publishing, *'Ford Cortina MKI'*, by Jonathan Wood.

...and three which are probably out of print:

Goodheart-Willcox Company, *'Automotive Body and Fender Repairs'* by C.E. Packer.

American Technical Society, *'Automotive Collision Work'*, by Edward D. Spicer.

Ure Smith, *'Panel Beating and Body Repairing'* by Donald Wait.

Plus at least a dozen different workshop manuals and owners' manuals for the Ford Cortina MKI.

Index

Tailpiece

Willow Publishing (Magor) hope that you have enjoyed this book and found it useful. If you have any comments or criticisms, we really want to hear from you, so write to the Publishers at, Barecroft Common, Magor, Newport, Gwent, NP6 3EB, United Kingdom.